Desktop Publishing: The Awful Truth

By Jeffery R. Parnau

19.95

Copyright ©1989 by Parnau Graphics, Inc. All Rights Reserved.
The reproduction or utilization of this work in any form by any electronic, mechanical, or other means, now known or hereafter invented, including photocopying or recording in any information storage and retrieval system is forbidden without the written permission of the publisher. First Printing, March 1989.

PARNAU GRAPHICS, INC.
P.O. Box 244
2857 S. 160th Street
New Berlin, Wisconsin, 53151 USA
(414) 784-7252
Printed in the United States of America

*Dedicated to whoever first said, Desktop Publishing Isn't.
With special thanks to Joanne, who actually read it three times.*

Contents

7 Introduction
15 The Sting
25 A Day in the Field
39 Mixed Marriages
47 How Do Publishers Publish?
61 What Does It Really Cost?
73 I Don't Know Art But . . .
83 DTP and Other Drugs
93 Output, the Great Equalizer
103 Doc, Will I Be Able to Play the Piano?
111 The Good News

Introduction

*"Be not the first by whom the new are tried,
nor yet the last to lay the old aside."*

— Alexander Pope

Let's get something straight, right up front. First of all, I am not "anti-Desktop Publishing." This book was created using software that you would probably describe as "Desktop Publishing" software. It was produced using Ventura Publisher version 2, proofed on an Apple Laserwriter, and set in final copy on conventional typesetting equipment using a code translation program.

Notice I said "created." *After* the book was created, it was published. Not using "Desktop Publishing" software, but using press releases, printing presses, paper, bindery equipment, and the telephone.

In other words: There is no such thing as "Desktop Publishing." And if you know what the word "publish" actually means, you know why many professionals gag at that awful buzzword (or, as I will henceforth abbreviate this misnomer, DTP). What we have seen over the past several years is merely a wave of typesetting and page makeup software which operates on small computers.

Professional publishers have always known the differences between setting type, putting a page together, and publishing a book. To publish something, you might write it, have it typeset, illustrated, and fully prepared . . . and *then* go ahead and publish it.

But there's something catchy about calling it DTP. It insinuates that the power of publishing has been unleashed to the masses, and now, with this computer and that software, anyone can "publish."

That is not true, and never will be. The truth is, many persons without publishing experience might now own and operate low-resolution typesetting equipment, but they are not publishing. They are setting type. They are doing electronic page assembly. They are using computer-assisted drawing programs. But they are not publishing.

Likewise, many professional publishers have installed DTP hardware and software, and are generating their own galleys and page proofs, rather than using an outside service. Because the pros have been dealing with typesetting evolution for decades, it came as no shock to see page

Introduction 9

makeup and typesetting software trickle down to personal computers.

But would the typical professional say that "We now publish on our own computers?" Hardly. He or she would say "We're setting type and doing page makeup on our computers."Not publishing.

What, then, is "the awful truth" about DTP? Primarily, the ommissions, exaggerations and lies perpetrated by those who manufacture and sell DTP hardware and software. While they can talk "ease," they forget to mention "quality." When they talk "photo," they forget to discuss "speed and resolution." When they say "complete," they neglect to mention "efficient."

That's no surprise. This is America, land of the free and home of the used car. It's not illegal to say that DTP can do anything and everything, and because that *isn't* illegal, it's being said. What's pathetic is that a small group of professionals, and a large group of non-professionals, swallow these exaggerations whole. They actually believe in used cars driven by little old ladies on Sundays, and that a $6,000 investment can make them a writer, proofreader, editor, artist, designer, and (why stop now) publisher — and as an added bonus, allow them to perform all of these jobs faster, more efficiently, and cheaper. And without training.

While it is true that there are certain "new" applications for DTP (what some have called "corporate publishing," which basically means making something look good that didn't used to have to look good but doing it anyhow *because you can*), this book will attempt do address DTP's abilities in the classic sense: real publishing.

That means we will examine DTP's ability to perform hyphenation, justification and page makeup. We'll measure its ability to incorporate graphic elements, photos, and color onto the page. We'll compare scanning on a low resolution, inexpensive machine to having photos prepared with conventional methods. We'll discuss how DTP output flows into the physical reproduction of the page — film preparation and printing. And we'll attempt to sort out its practical abilities from those which are impractical, but available to those who don't know any better.

Why pick on publishers?

A question I've often pondered over the years is this: Why do the typesetting manufacturers first sell their new wares to the publishers, and later to the typesetting firms and service bureaus?

And I've always answered it the same way, as have my professional colleagues. Because the industry knows better.

This classic scenario occurred thousands of times as DTP began to emerge. We in the typesetting business were the first in line to see the demonstrations. But we always asked the wrong questions. For example, we might say, "Can you line that up like this, and move this over by a point, because my customer would go nuts if I did that." And that comment might cause the entire system to crash. Or it might take 45 minutes to make the change. Upon seeing that, the professional would meander over to the next booth, or turn the page, or whatever.

Now look at the person who does not set type or perform page makeup, but who thinks those services are overpriced. If he or she is not in the business of type, can he or she ask the right questions? Sort out the hype, the exaggeration, the lies?

The result has been consistent over the years. Before IBM ever sold a strike-on "composer" to a type house, they sold them to publishers. Before IBM sold its beastly Magnetic Tape Composition System to a professional, it was sold to a publisher who wanted to "save money" by setting type.

Before a profitable typesetting firm ever even dreamed of buying a limited table-top phototypesetter with no long-term storage, no memory, and two fonts, a publisher who had never set a lick of type already owned one.

It's only natural. And it's a mistake I personally made while working for publishers. In the mid 1970's, I scrapped a complete IBM strike-on system for a new-fangled floppy disk system. Our publishing company had been one of the first users of both systems. Why did we buy the first? To get more control, run later deadlines, and save money. Why the second? Because the first was so slow, unprofitable, and costly. We had to either upgrade, or get out of the business.

On the other hand, I was never one to trust typesetting firms. Obviously, people are in that business to make money. It makes sense for a person who makes a living by selling me type to tell me to stay out of the business. So I never listened to anyone but my publisher and myself. We continued to stay on the leading edge of technology, as we saw it. (As others saw it, we continued to desperately purchase every new low-end system, and never gave up hoping that it would eventually become easy, pleasant, and profitable.)

DTP followed a predictable course. Professional typesetting firms tried it in the early stages and temporarily scrapped it. Publishers — typically those who were not already in the business of setting type — bought it. Now, as it matures, the professionals are picking and choosing from DTP abilities, while the front-running, experimental publishers are trying to generate complete projects, incorporating photos, charts, and color separations into their little machines.

You don't have to trust me, but at least give this some thought: Professionals in the typesetting and film preparation business are accustomed to rapid change, and are always open to new equipment and ideas. This end of the "publication business" has always been highly competitive, and the pros are always looking for ways to get ahead, to do it faster, to sell it cheaper than the competition can produce it. If you're looking at new technology that the professionals have shunned, find out why. And I do not mean to suggest that the professionals have shunned DTP itself. But if your film house is not scanning photos, do yourself a favor. Before you run out and purchase a scanner to "save money and get it done faster and better," find out why the film house hasn't ordered one. They just might know something you don't — like how long the process takes, how much computer storage it requires, and whether it provides immediate or long-term benefits.

Introduction **13**

The DTP shopper

If this book simply makes you a better DTP shopper, it's done its job. True, it is not likely that you will read this book and then rush out to purchase a scanner, a color separation system, and an optical character reader. But the fact is, some DTP tools are simply not required by 99.9 percent of us. Some things just don't work well yet. Other DTP equipment and software is quite intriguing, and useful in many publishing applications.

My goal is not to convince you to avoid DTP systems. Rather, my goal is to make sure you don't buy things that don't work, or don't work the way you *think* they will work.

Chapter 1:

The Sting

You've seen them. Those television commercials in which one harried executive discovers the secret of another executive's productivity. He flips through a report filled with bar graphs and pie charts, with wrapped copy and a galaxy of typefaces. He speaks in a hushed tone.

"How long did this take your staff?" he asks quietly. "A couple of months?"

"We did it in a week," the other casually replies. Fade to black . . . and there it is: the Macintosh logo.

It's certainly true that you can produce a slick-looking business presentation or annual report via DTP techniques. It may even be true that a small department can produce such a job in a week. But a "report" is typically assembled by a very small staff — possibly even a lone worker. And slick business reports are not necessarily published on a predictable schedule.

To add to the confusion, some industry observers are beginning to break all of this "publishing stuff" into sub-categories. That business report might have fallen into the new category of "corporate publishing" -- or, if it included a slide presentation, it may have been classified as "presentation graphics." And as the industry defines these fragmentations, special software pops up to handle each reinvented need.

The point: That TV ad shows a special case — the business report created by a small staff in a short time — and urges you to believe that, using that same approach, you can "publish" anything this can be done regularly. And you can produce it as regularly as a newsletter, or newspaper, or magazine. You can do it without typesetters, printers, paste-up artists, and all those others who are after your money. You can do it all with this little box.

That's the siren-song of the desktop sales force, and it has seduced many publishers — but even more would-be "publishers" who treat a computer as the ticket to publishing heaven.

"Produce a full-page ad in just an hour," they hear.

"Eliminate typesetting, galleys, and pasteup, even scissors, wax and glue in most cases."

"Make your publications more competitive and profitable — all for an initial investment of less than $6,000."

Oh, really?

Telling the tale

One of the advocates publishers have read is Donna Munari, who wrote an article called "Discovering the Secrets of Desktop Publishing" in the November/December 1988 issue of the industry trade journal *Successful*

Magazine Publishing. This one article contains virtually every element DTP advocates use to seduce "publishers" into that "initial investment." In fact, the three quotes used above are taken directly from her article.

Here is the tale she tells:

"DTP dramatically reduces the time spent on producing pages, allowing you to publish on schedule," she says. DTP's flexibility gives you the freedom to make eleventh hour layout changes. And "creative control is an important benefit of DTP" because the production function is brought in-house.

(Wait a minute. If you currently purchase your "pages" from an outside vendor, as insinuated, how does DTP dramatically reduce the time you spend on a page? Doesn't this statement suggest that you will be spending *more* time on a page?)

"With one Apple Macintosh (Mac), you could produce a monthly 64-128 page magazine . . . . In the downtime, you might be able to produce brochures and newsletters." Why, you could even "bring a Mac to your convention to put out a daily convention newsletter!"

(Hold on! Isn't it true that only one person can work on one Mac at one time? Doesn't this statement suggest that a single person can produce 128 pages of magazine material a month? And doesn't it go on to say that this one-person, one-computer publishing company will also have time to produce brochures and newsletters?)

"Forty-two percent of the respondents to a February 1988 ASAE [American Society of Association Executives] survey in the D.C. area currently use DTP; another 34 percent plan to purchase a system within the next two years."

(What? Does that mean that three out of four respondents to the *average* survey are buying DTP equipment?

The hook

Let's examine these claims in further detail. Can DTP keep you on schedule? Only if you *already* stay on your publishing on schedule. It can't force you to meet deadlines, so either you'll meet them or not, "just like usual."

And while DTP may decrease the time spent making pages, it's now *your* time (or your staff's) that's used in making the pages. Any "eleventh hour" changes you decide to make will cost you even *more* time — just as they'd have cost you money for the extra time the folks at the service house would have to put in. Only you can answer the question as to which is more important — your time or your money. DTP doesn't answer that for you.

Just one Mac can "produce" a 128-page magazine? Who is she trying to kid? Is this that same $6,000 initial-investment Mac? What does she mean by "produce?" Certainly she couldn't mean that one Mac can do layout, typesetting, and film preparation for a 128-page, typical monthly magazine. (But that's what she said.) And even if it could, how would you get "hard copy"? How does the Mac turn its pretty screens of layout into cold hard pages?

As it turns out, this question of output is never addressed in the entire article. That's a common ploy in the DTP pitch, because if you found out what it would cost you (both in time and money) to get single color or (gulp) four-color films from your Mac you'd run screaming into the night. But we'll get to that later.

Oh, yeah — the business about creating a convention newsletter. Again, how would you output the typesetting for the newsletter? Borrow a laser printer? Okay, for a low-end model that means you can create a one-page, 8 1/2 x 11 inch newsletter printed on one side — at a rate of one page every 15 seconds. If you want to print on both sides, you'll have to run your pages through the laser printer again. You could speed things up by photocopying the "newsletter," but since you have no means of binding the job you're still restricted to a one-page format.

True, I'm being catty. But bear in mind, I'm not the one who likes to use the term desktop *publisher*. Although that word implies that someone is arranging for the printing, binding, and distribution of a publication, the sirens of DTP rarely, if ever, remind you that to publish, you must output and print.

And gee, forty-two percent of the respondents to a survey in the Washington, D.C., area use DTP — and another third plan to! Where's the catch in the statistics? It was a survey of Association Executives. A group which, by nature, must publish a newsletter. That might be four pages a month. Or more or less.

The sting

Amidst all the hyperbole in the claims of DTP advocates, nothing reveals the true state of the art like the question of output. How do you get what's on the screen onto paper or film? Laser printer? Unless you're willing to pay upwards of $4,000 (that's in addition to your initial investment of six G's), the type and graphics you produce will not be of publication quality. And at $4,000, most professionals would say that you are getting only low-resolution proofs. Something a pro might never allow to go to press.

Of course, you could always purchase a Linotype laser typesetter. With a resolution over 1200 dots per inch and the ability to draw on film as well as paper, one of these machines will easily produce whole pages of publication-quality text, line art, and tints. Cost? Figure $80,000. But will it be able to output your photos? Not yet. You need a scanner for that. $2,500 for something that will generate useless, low-resolution photos. $20,000 for something that might give you a photo, but require several 278 megabyte hard drives for storage. Or $100,000 for the only unit on the market that does a good black-and-white photo, and is "almost" ready to output that material in a DTP compatible format.

Even the self-proclaimed magazine of DTP, *Publish!*, which prides itself in being produced via desktop techniques, admits that not everything can be done with DTP. Among the impressive list of hardware and software used to produce the magazine, you'll find the telling phrase, "Photographs and some illustrations were produced conventionally." Why? Apparently, in early 1989, most photos and "some" graphics just don't come popping out of little computers, no matter how much a DTP publisher wants it to happen.

So be warned. DTP is not "the complete solution to all your publishing problems" (as, believe it or not, one DTP manufacturer describes his product). For that matter, DTP, handled without forethought, is simply one *more* publishing problem.

Likewise, be ready. If you pay as much attention to what the professionals are doing as you pay to the DTP sirens, you'll see myths slowly melt into realities. While the hype surrounding DTP will certainly fade, the techniques it uses are the same techniques we've seen emerging in the publishing industry for years.

Given a few more radical developments in PC disk-memory capacity and processing speed, we may see the promise of DTP emerge as an affordable, practical, and universally capable system. Until then, the professionals will use it piecemeal. If something works, great. If not, we've got the old methods.

Where are the complaints?

There is one final consideration to "The Sting." How come those who have purchased systems that don't deliver just sit quietly by, suffering through their situation?

Think about this. Suppose I work for a small company, and I propose that in order to save lots of money, get our work done faster, and become more efficient, we purchase three computers, a laser printer, and switch to an outside vendor who can run our material in high-resolution. So that's what we do.

For six months, I struggle with training and testing, and whenever I beg for help, I'm told by the salesman that this is a normal learning curve, and that things will smooth out. At the end of nine months, I've got too much manpower and equipment and training committed to the project. So I don't give it further thought. I *must* make it work.

But what if I'm a high-level manager, and I decide to give limited approval to the above project? And at the end of nine months, I evaluate the results, and determine that it was a bad idea? I'll get a few points for tossing the equipment out, firing the idiot who bought it, and writing a scathing report.

I have personally seen the above situations occur many times. The person who decided that DTP would solve "all of our publishing problems" is the last one to admit that something isn't working, or that he got sold a bill of goods. His reputation is at stake. And his or her boss, maintaining a critical distance, will be the one to toss the whole mess out, regardless of equipment or cost. I've seen $50,000 systems trashed in order to save money the old fashioned way, and I've seen $25,000 systems plod along at half the speed of the methods they replaced. It's as political as it is business-wise.

So typically, either you are committed to making DTP work regardless, or you somehow maintain your distance, and critically evaluate it — even if it means admitting you expected too much too soon, or fell for some big black lie. Chances are, the lower you are on the managerial level, the more tempted you will be to plod on with DTP, right or wrong. And that's the sting.

Summary

- Advertisements, people, and your own desires may lead you to be seduced by ridiculous, impossible claims about artwork, typesetting, or other related skills.
- An individual cannot be expected to both implement and objectively evaluate a system at the same time.
- DTP systems have certain advantages over conventional systems, but only in certain situations. The opposite is true in other cases.

Chapter 2:

A Day in the Field

Actually, we are going to spend more than one day in the field. We'll visit several DTP users, and find out what works. And what doesn't work. And whether they've had problems, or things pretty much did what they were supposed to do.

We'll visit not only different users, but users who use DTP differently. One is an artist — a designer who now makes his living illustrating on his Macintosh, and teaching others how to use Macintoshes for illustration. We'll visit with a person who functions as a combination art-director/pasteup/typesetter, but whose former strength (pre-DTP) was in art direction and illustration. We'll visit with a firm that publishes a magazine using one IBM compatible. And we'll visit with a film house manager who's trying to figure out what to do next.

The art director/typesetter

J.H. is a jovial, genuinely nice guy who's new to working as a professional in the publishing business. He works for himself, freelancing to ad agencies, magazine publishers, and other firms. He does all of his work on a Macintosh, which is equipped with a 60 megabyte hard drive, a standard 3-1/2 inch drive, 8 megabytes of memory, a modem, a Laserwriter, an 8-1/2 x 11 inch flat scanner, and a 21-inch, full color monitor.

JP: Tell me, how did you get into DTP?

JH: Well, I always wanted to get into art direction full time. About three years ago, I quit my former job and now do it for a living. I started out on the Macintosh. I was one of the first full-time art directors in the midwest to do that.

JP: How do you like the Macintosh?

JH: It's the present, the future, man, it's everything. It's where the industry is going.

JP: You have a pretty expensive setup. Eight megabytes of memory alone, that's about $4,000, isn't it?

JH: One thing you gotta understand. That machine, when you buy it, it's just an empty box. It's a piggy bank. All you do is put money in it. Eight meg of memory is nothing. My big problem is I *always* run out of memory. I can stick more in, and I probably will.

JP: You have a scanner. What do you use it for?

JH: Lots of times when I'm doing a page, I might scan the photos, and blow them up, and be able to put out a proof on the Laserwriter, and it's quite sophisticated. It looks great.

A Day in the Field

JP: Why not just sketch the photos onto the layouts by hand?

JH: I do that too. I have a pretty good hand. It depends on what the customer wants to see, what they're paying me to do. If I want to work fast, I just use a pencil.

JP: What about stretching and fitting a scanned photo. Do you ever use that ability?

JH: I play with it. But you can't really use it on most jobs. This scanner here, this doesn't produce something you would ever print. It doesn't have any resolution. It's just rough stuff. So, if I were to stretch a photo sideways or something, that's easy for me, but how would they do it later when they wanted final output quality?

JP: What about an occasional photo? I've read that scanners are hot. Do you use it once in a while for final output on a brochure or something?

JH: No. This only cost $2,500, and nobody would want to see one of these scans in print. They're just for the screen or for a rough proof.

JP: How are your pages finally output?

JH: On an L-300 Mergenthaler Linotronic.

JP: To paper or film?

JH: We go right to film. We do enough proofs here to get it right, so by the time we need final output, we go right to film.

JP: I noticed that you use an extremely fine tint on some panels. Why is that? And what is it? It looks like about a 3% tint to me.

JH: No, we got a problem in moving from the laser proof to the final quality machine. Believe it or not, on the laser proof, that's a 30 percent tint, and it looks way too dark. On the Linotronic it comes out so you can hardly see it.

JP: Why is that?

JH: I don't know. Nobody seems to know. We got the same kind of problem with color.

JP: What is that problem?

JH: Well on the Macintosh, you can mix PMS colors, and you can mix tints. You can pretty much do anything you want. For example you can take 20 percent yellow and 20 percent magenta and mix a little pink. Well, you can go mix colors all you want and get it looking great on the screen. But then you get the film from the L-300, and they make the color proof, and it is a totally different color.

JP: So how do you get the color mix that you really want?

JH: It's a bug. They have to fix it. Right now, I couldn't tell you exactly how to do it.

JP: I was studying your printed samples. I was curious, do you draw a box one line at a time? Or two sides at a time? I noticed that on all of your boxes, the horizontal rules and the vertical rules are of two different thicknesses. Do you do that on purpose?

JH: No. I understand it is because our rules are so thin that when the program converts from 300 lines per inch to 1200 lines per inch, it can make minor mistakes in the Y calculation compared to the X calculation. It's nothing I can control, unless I make the rules thicker. Nobody ever noticed it before you did except me.

A Day in the Field **29**

JP: Thanks. I'll take that as a compliment to my keen sense of balance. Back to this thing about colors not matching. Doesn't that bother you?

JH: Well sure. It's a big problem. But hell, we have lots of problems in this business. This is just the beginning of a whole revolution.

JP: Could you think, offhand, of other areas that have given you either pleasant or unpleasant surprises?

JH: Well on the pleasant side, I wouldn't be doing this for a living if it didn't make sense. Like I said, this is the future. But on the problem side, some pretty weird stuff happens with tints. As I understand our printer, there's something unusual about the shape of our film dot. It's not round, not square. I guess it's not even in a certain screen. All of the tints are supposed to be 133 line, but there's some sort of problem that makes them go finer than that. That I could live with. The stuff that bothers me with the tints is that we can't control the ability of the output machine. Sometimes a fine hairline goes all the way down the middle of a tint, like the machine just jumped off the track at that point. It might go right through the type.

JP: What about registration? Looking at your printed samples, I notice that when you fill a box with a color panel, you don't, for example, make the color slightly overlap into a black rule.

JH: There's two problems there. One, printing technology has got to catch up to desktop publishing technology. The average press is always going out of register. And two, that's something that I can't fix. If I say, "fill that box," the program runs the color right up to the line. I can't make it get a little bigger. They say they're going to add that ability in the next version, because printers have been having problems with it.

JP: Well, I think maybe desktop technology ought to pay a little more attention to the rules we have in printing. We were here first, you know.

JH: Yeah, I know. But printing is a sloppy art. It really ought to tighten up its act.

JP: On this spread here, this two-pager, I notice you drew the boxes at angles, and sort of cocked the type to make it look like its going up hill. Did that take more time?

JH: You know it did or you wouldn't ask. Yeah. I'd say those two pages took me eight hours to design and lay out.

JP: How could they take that long? It's just a couple of headings and captions, and four boxes with shadows.

JH: You probably know darn well why. One program, I use for designing the two-page spread, and with that program, any type or boxes that go in normally can be drawn. That's the program I use for most pages. Another thing, I'm a designer. I do a lot of testing, so maybe I ran ten proofs or so, and then modified them. But the big penalty was in having to use an illustration program to put the boxes and type at the angles, and then save each caption and each box as an art element. Then you go back to the main program and import them as art elements, one at a time. It takes time. But it's what the customer was looking for, and that's what it takes to do it.

JP: Wouldn't that have been faster on a drawing board?

JH: Probably. But I don't work on a drawing board for two pages, and go back to the computer for the next two.

JP: I've heard that sometimes you can draw something with one program in one resolution, say 133 line, and if you import it to another program, you might lose all of the detail, and it could default to 65 line. Is that possible?

JH: We've had that problem. You have to be aware of the limitations, of the compatibility between programs. Just because you draw something with one doesn't mean you can import it into another with the same colors or resolutions. You have to either have fully compatible software, or understand how one program will interpret the output of another.

JP: How do you learn that?

JH: I just experiment. Eventually you learn it. Trial and error, mostly.

JP: What about speed? I know that sometimes output speeds are slow, depending on how much you've used photos and tints and graphic elements. Have you had problems there?

JH: The worst was once, I scanned this photo, and was going to run a laser proof. I couldn't tell after while if the laser was hung up or if it was still trying to run the photo, so I turned the whole system off. It fried my hard disk doing that, and I had to restore everything. So I don't know. I try not to run things that I know will take too much time.

The prep house

Barry owns a magazine film preparation house. Several of his customers now send him film generated on the Linotronic L-300. He's thinking of adding a PostScript typesetting device to his own shop.

JP: Why do you think you want to add a PostScript device?

BD: I don't, really. But I get about one call a week from someone asking if we can accept PostScript files. Two of our customers now send their jobs in with the type and color breaks on film.

JP: Do you like it that way?

BD: Well, I don't really care as long as everything fits and makes sense. But I'd rather be making money generating that film in here, which is one reason I want to consider adding the laser device.

JP: What would you charge for a page?

BD: We'd try to follow the norm, which is $8 to $12 per page per color.

JP: So if a person ran a page that used all four colors, the page could cost up to $48 just to run as film? And no less than $32? Isn't that high?

BD: It's what people charge.

JP: What about halftones. How would you handle them?

BD: Conventionally. Nobody is scanning them, if that's what you mean. It doesn't make sense to do that.

JP: The same with color?

BD: Right. We scan the color on a regular scanner, a litho scanner. Same kind of scanner we've been using for years.

JP: Has the quality of the material improved or gotten worse for those customers who are supplying L-300 film?

BD: Well, it's not worse. It's just that sometimes they don't understand what they can and cannot do. Like this one guy sends us four negs, with this four-color illustration that looks like a separation of air-brushed clouds, and the edges of the art fade out to nothing. He wants us to reverse this out of a color separation. You can't do that. That's the biggest problem. Once they see that film, they think their troubles are over. For us, that's where they start.

JP: I've heard that sometimes supplied film doesn't fit, that it doesn't register. Is that true?

BD: Not any more. I think it was an early problem, but we haven't seen it lately at all.

JP: Have you run into any new or unique situations with supplied film from these customers?

BD: Yes. The worst part is corrections or alterations. Obviously, if we receive a negative for the black, and the customer ran a tint in the background, and then wants us to change some of the type after they see a proof, we're dead. We can't make type changes. The only way to get a change made is for them to supply another neg. And you'd be surprised at how they pretend not to know that. Usually, the big problems will be related somehow to tints mixed with type somewhere. Or another one, where the customer runs a thin one-point rule around a photo, and wants the rule to be composed of three tints, but when we spread the photo into the rule, the rule disappears. Just weird problems that we didn't run into before.

JP: Do you solve them as they arise?

BD: When we can. Sometimes we say, "Never do that again." Sometimes we just explain the situation, and have them send four new negatives. Obviously, if we knew where the errors were going to come from we'd tell the customer before the errors occurred. It's a learning experience. We see something new every day. It's one more reason we want the ability to run the negs right here.

JP: Do you consider it cost effective for customers to go right to the negs on the L-300?

BD: It's hard to say. It's a machine with overhead. I figure we have to run 12,000 pages on it to break even, assuming we charge $8 a page. It's not like a $5,000 camera. On the other hand, it doesn't take a trained person to turn it on and stick a disk in a slot and get full page, separated negs.

JP: So you've decided to order a machine for sure?

BD: Not yet. One, we might go with the L-500. Two, we're looking at the Birmysetter, the Compugraphic, and the new low-end Linotronic. Three, we need to see a little more action. So far I haven't really lost current business to anyone who's running laser film. I almost want to see that happen first. I don't want to be the first guy on our block to say I shouldn't have bought one of these things.

JP: What about the plus side of it all?

BD: Obviously this is where the industry is going, and we want to go there too. It's our business. On the plus side, when it's all working, I want one. I'll wait as long as makes sense, and then I'll get one.

JP: Why are you so sure this is where the industry is going?

BD: It's the only big movement I see. Everybody talks about PostScript, about the L-300, about going to film. If anything else is out there, it isn't being talked about.

The illustrator

Steve is an independent illustrator who had formal training in art, and only recently decided to dedicate his professional time to the Macintosh as an art tool.

JP: Why the decision to use the Macintosh for illustration?

SB: It's the future. It's how artists and designers will translate their thoughts and ideas into reproducable information. And it's fun.

JP: Your work looks great. But to be blunt, I would hate to try to reproduce it, to print it. On this piece, you use six PMS colors, and all of the registration is kiss or butt.

SB: I know. That's one of the limitations that they're working on all the time. They should have something for it pretty soon.

JP: Steve, if you know this is almost impossible to print, can't you do something to make it more practical?

SB: Well, it's difficult to print I admit. But that's also part of what makes it so beautiful when it's finished. It's technically an amazing piece in that it shows lithography running at its best, and in part, that is what the piece is attempting to convey. The best of DTP, the best of lithography, and the best of me.

The publisher

Tom and his crew produce a bimonthly magazine, typically 112 pages, with a conventional mix of advertising and editorial. They use an IBM compatible, AT-class machine.

JP: You're using Aldus Pagemaker for the IBM PC. How do you like it?

TM: We're not too happy with it. We're thinking of upgrading the machine to a 386. The problem is, it's slow.

JP: Compared to what?

TM: We were using Ventura Publisher version 1.1. For some reason we decided to move over to Pagemaker. But we're spending too much time staring at the screen, waiting for stuff to happen. We heard now that Ventura version 2 has better typographic control, and runs pretty fast, so we've ordered that, and we're looking forward to trying it out.

JP: You're using a full-page monitor. Do you recommend that?

TM: Definitely. The cost isn't that significant any more. We can buy one of these for $1,300, while they used to be $2,000. All that scrolling around is crazy. You have to go full page.

JP: Looking at your pasteup boards, I see that you get the type set as full pages, but then add photostats, move things around, paste corrections over type. Is that normal?

TM: We were never looking to become, quote, desktop publishers. Our problem was we would have liked to set type in house, but we didn't want to spend the money on the equipment. The way we work now, we send disks over to our typesetting house, and they run pages for us. From that point on, we treat the book the same way we used to.

JP: How does the type house like that?

TM: We were sort of instrumental in recommending they put in the L-300 and begin to offer output services.

JP: Are they happy?

TM: Well, it was sort of a surprise for them. Up until then, the owner said he never had to market typesetting, that customers just came to him. Now, he says he has to educate people in going the DTP route, and having them run pages at $8 a crack. It's been a difficult transition. He's lost a lot of work to the low-resolution machines, customers who don't really need the high quality. I hope he survives.

JP: Do you plan to add halftone ability or color ability?

TM: No. As I said, we want to set type, and being able to set it as full pages, to proof it, to correct it, and then to get it run a few miles from here, that's great. That's all we want. In the future we'll see what happens.

JP: What about training? Did you train a current art director to transition to this? Or an editor?

TM: Our designer works on the terminal. He had no experience on a computer before this. The only problem we have with him is that he's very, very dependent on the user interface, or the mouse. He can point and click, but like he says, "If I can't click it, I can't do it."

JP: Does that present a problem?

TM: No, not really. He's limited to working on pages, but that's what we pay him for. I guess it's not really a problem. Just an observation.

JP: What do you see as your next step?

TM: This probably sounds repetitive, but we just got to where we've wanted to be for a long time. We ought to be fine for a while. Maybe we'll add another computer. But things are going very nicely.

JP: I've interviewed several people who use DTP, and I've heard of a lot of problems. What have you experienced?

TM: None other than what I mentioned. We might go back to Ventura. But that's not a problem, that's just a switch in software. We've got the Laserwriter and the AT, and we have a vendor who runs final pages. We don't have problems. These are solutions.

JP: No problems?

TM: Really, no problem. I think we investigated this stuff properly. We're not trying to win DTP design contests. We're not trying to scan halftones. All we're doing is trying to get our proofs as full pages of type, and to get our type run after it's what we want. This is something we've wanted to do, and we installed it, and it's working well. We've come a long way and we'll make changes as we see fit, but we're very happy with this setup.

Summary

- Expect to uncover problems in installing any DTP system, some of which you may be the first to discover, and not all of which can be resolved. You may have to compromise.
- Those with a non-publishing background tend to have the highest expectations for DTP, and without exposure to conventional systems, do not instinctively recognize their own successes or failures.
- Companies which make the most specific, limited use of DTP tend to be those who are having the most success with it, and are the most happy using it.

Chapter 3:

Mixed Marriages

The DTP salesman is grinning at you, a little of the gold on one of his teeth sparkling in the soft glow of the computer terminal. "Compatible? You betcha. Compatible with everything. Just plug it all in and let it fly."

Sounds a bit fishy, doesn't it? Let's take a look at the hardware and software in use by the staff of a single magazine which, as it happens, focuses on the field of DTP.

Under the caption titled "tools used to produce this issue," they list the following software:

Microsoft Word, Appleshare, Microphone, Maclink, Lap Link, Capture, Pagemaker, Letr Tuck, Fontographer, Adobe Illustrator 88, Freehand, Adobe Separator, Laserpaint Color II.

Of course, that software has to run on some hardware. Again, to produce that single 112 page issue, they used:

Macintosh Plus, Macintosh II, Macintosh IIx, and Macintosh SE computers, Dataframe XP hard disks, a

Compaq Deskpro 386, an IBM PC AT, a Microtek 300G scanner, a Hayes Interbridge, a Laserwriter II-NTX with a Dataframe hard disk, and a Linotronic 300.

(They mention also that the photos were handled conventionally, as were "some" illustrations. Seems like a lot of firepower, and still they don't do the photos on the DTP system?)

This magazine doesn't say that they simply plugged it all in and it worked like a top. Nor does it suggest that one little guy did the whole magazine by himself, bouncing from one computer to the next, from one piece of software to the next, from one laser device to another.

What's required?

Does it really take 11 pieces of hardware and 13 different programs to make DTP work? Of course not. But if your magazine specializes in DTP, you get to play with all kinds of stuff. Playing is part of the job.

On the other hand, just how easy is it to get all of that software to work, in concert, on the hardware? And how come no mention of Ventura Publisher? They have PCs, don't they?

Let's start with the great wall. It is the wall between pagination programs. If you use Pagemaker, then your pages are stored, eventually, for Pagemaker. It is absurd to think that you would take a Pagemaker file from one computer, and then load it onto a computer which uses Ventura. You simply make a decision. You work with a single, "unifying" program or environment.

After making that choice, you start to use the mechanic's credo. Anything can be made to fit anywhere, if you have a big enough hammer. In other words, although one piece of software might not work comfortably or easily with another one, rest assured that with enough patience and effort, you will get some sort of results. Maybe not what you wanted, expected, or can use, but generally, at least something for your efforts.

Incompatibility

In interviewing DTP users for this book, we came across some confusing, if not disturbing, software and hardware conflicts. Each time we found a conflict, it was described to us as unexpected, undocumented, and user-discovered. Of course, there is no way to prove that: The DTP user expects only what he has read about, and many computer users skip half or more of each operation manual they own.

Here, though, is a typical example of the kind of conflict we saw. A designer in the firm was using an illustration program to generate a complex drawing. It was an interesting graphic shape based on repeating and rotating a rectangle. The rectangle itself was electronically airbrushed. We were viewing this on his 21-inch monitor when another DTP artist walked by. He began to chuckle.

"You know, you can't import that into Quark."

"Why not?" my friend asked.

"You'll lose all that detail. You'll drop down to low resolution when you transfer it."

"Why?"

"It just will. I don't know why."

They discussed the details for a few minutes. The artist who gave the warning related how he had tried to use these two programs together, but could not make them work in concert. Each time he "exported" a drawing from the drawing program to the "page" program, detail and resolution were lost. He investigated it, and found that there were special programs which should allow him to preserve the data, but he hadn't had the time to try them. And he was angry that the supplier of the DTP program never addressed this particular problem of incompability.

And so, after spending hours creating the illustration, all my friend could do was shake his head, saying, "Why don't they put that in the manual somewhere?"

They probably do, somewhere, along with a list of other things that come and go as you move data from one program to another. But remember, each individual company which produces software is under no obligation to make these transfers easy, or even possible. What's the answer? Careful shopping. Get a demonstration before you buy. Don't trust the sales persons; they may not know any more than you do about what you're buying.

DTP life on the edge: Examples

Let's take a look at some of the problems that have been reported by DTP users when they start mixing one program with another. Some of these are paraphrased summaries of questions that were answered in lengthy technical detail in trade magazines. Some are based on personal experiences, and the balance on the frustrations of acquaintances.

Mixed Marriages

- **Lost images.** The DTP user imported graphic images into a layout, and then copied the job to a portable computer, and then tried to have final, high-resolution output generated. The program could not handle "copied" files. This is one of the more bizarre, unexpected types of problem that confuse even highly experienced computer operators.

- **One Mac to another.** The word spacing that shows up on one Mac is different from that seen when viewing the same, unmodified file on a different Mac. While several DTP experts explain how to "work around" the problem, they can't explain why it occurs. But they agree that it is a problem.

- **Page size.** How large an area can a Laserwriter print? On an 8.5 by 11 inch sheet, it can print up to 8 by 10.5 inches in one mode, or up to 7.6 by 10.1 inches in another mode . . . unless it is using Aldus Pagemaker which is using Aldus Prep files, in which case it can print to 8 by 10.9 inches. But if it is using the Mac Laser Prep file, you must use the smallest size if you plan to download fonts, because that saves you 100K of Laserwriter memory. If that all sounds confusing, don't feel bad. It's nuts.

- **Memory and VP.** Ventura Publisher needs most of the typical 640K that a basic AT can address directly. But if the user has a mouse that has a driver that is a little larger than the VP people anticipated, you may get a screen warning that advises you to use a different loading parameter to free up some memory. That is your only alternative in some cases — along with the warning that "some printers may not work" once you do that. The same warning becomes the rule if you use, as the manual suggests, a disk cache.

- **Lost math.** Doing equations in Microsoft Word, this DTP user found that their math formats were lost when he transferred the files to Pagemaker. Solution: Purchase one of two other pieces of software designed to solve the problem.
- **How many fonts?** The Laserwriter doesn't have all of its fonts in it when you turn it on. They must be downloaded, typically once a day. How many can you download? On his Laserwriter II, this user found out his machine had about 395K of its 512K available for fonts, but that 290K was a good limit. A single 24 point font might consume 100K. But even if all of the fonts were of the tiny 15K size, the max for this machine was 32 fonts, with a theoretical max in certain cases of only two fonts.
- **Lost formats.** Can a Mindwrite file be imported into Pagemaker? Sure, if the user is a member of Compuserve, and finds the filter program from Access Technology. Otherwise, he might convert them to Macwrite, but that would destroy paragraph numbering.
- **Technobabble.** This DTP user complained that when he connected his Laserwriter II SC to his Mac Plus with a Photon 30 hard drive by Warp 9, the printer and hard disk would not run together. The solution: Send the drive back to the manufacturer and get it upgraded.
- **Screen fonts ugly.** Why do certain Ventura fonts on the IBM look good, and others bad? Because they're sort of created on the fly, and don't really exist in all sizes. The solution, offered by one DTP writer, was a seven step exercise using DOS's Debug program.
- **No fonts.** This novice thought that all service bureaus purchased all fonts. When he had his pages run in high resolution, he found that his fancy, store-bought font ap-

peared as the typewriter face, Courier. His service bureau, not wanting to investigate the matter further, told him to take his business elsewhere.
- **Uglier still.** This Mac user found that above 24 point, some of his text was unreadable and difficult to space properly. Solution: Purchase and install a program called Font Sizer.
- **Wrong fonts.** This user found that although the Laserwriter proofs were fine, and everything seemed okay, that the output from his service bureau came back with all different fonts. He learned that the early DTP thinkers didn't plan on that many fonts and ran out of numbers. So now, he has to be sure to coordinate font numbers with his service bureau.
- **Importation problems.** This general category has to do with getting one drawing format into a program that prefers another format. The tricks, tips, and suggestions that allow you to achieve your dubious goal sometimes require the purchase of still a third program, and that the drawing be edited or cropped. With over a dozen drawing formats out there, this could be the biggest area of confusion in the DTP field.

Who learns it all?

Is that all? Far from it. There are hundreds of DTP products on the market, and making any one of them work with another might require the purchase of another still.

Back to our opening example, who in the operation would actually know how to operate 13 pieces of complicated software on 11 different pieces of hardware? How long would it take to train for that kind of environment?

Don't be foolish. When you talk about a department of that size and complexity, you'll require at least several persons who are functional experts in different areas with different equipment. For that matter, if you want to use the complex, color illustration programs, you'll need a complex, colorful artist on the staff — one who likes to work with computers.

But that installation is pretty rare. More typical will be the single-or several-machine environment, with several basic software packages: word processor, pagination program, and possibly a simple drawing program.

If your ultimate goal is the Great Desktop Lie — "Do it all with DTP" — you'll no doubt be shaken, at first, at the problems you'll encounter moving even simple material from one program or device to another. Once you step beyond that magic door called Graphics, you're pretty much on your own.

Summary

- DTP compatibility problems generally arise when you decide to use a specialty program for one task, and to export your work to another program which does not specifically support your mix.
- There is a legitimate software "underground" that specializes in making programs and machines talk to each other, and in helping the user control the dozens of text and graphic file formats in use today.
- The only sure way to know if what you want to do is actually possible is to see it in action. Don't buy on promises. If the sales force can't show it to you, assume (to be safe) that it can't be done.

Chapter 4:

How do Publishers Publish?

If you picked up an issue of *Publish!* magazine and leafed through it, and then walked through the typical publishing office, you might find yourself wondering, "Hey, where's all the equipment I just read about? How do you people publish?"

Another person might be even more naive. I got a call from a young fellow. He said he was going to start publishing a magazine. He bought a Macintosh and a Laserwriter, and he was about ready to start this here "publishing," and he wanted some tips, like "How should I get it printed? How many should I print? How do you sell advertising? Where should I buy a mailing list? Can it be sold on newsstands, and do you think I should do my own list maintenance?"

Other than those few areas, he pretty well had publishing all figured out.

Of course, magazines, books, catalogs, and newspapers have been "published" for centuries. DTP didn't make it all happen, as some of the novices to publishing seem to think.

So how does the typical, real, long-term publisher actually — wait, wait! We have to get rid of that darn buzzword again. The typical publisher publishes by printing things and distributing them. Or, more precisely, by arranging for the printing and distribution of material. It takes paper and ink and presses and trucks to really publish something. Sometimes, when I think too long about DTP, I forget that myself.

What you really might be wondering is, "How do publishers set type? How do you get a picture on the page? How do you handle advertising? How do you pack it all up and ship it to your printer?"

Obviously, all of this was going on prior to the DTP "revolution" in 1985. Not so obviously, most of it is still going on in much the same fashion as it was then. And the larger the operation, the further it probably is from using DTP technology. So let's review how today's typical publisher handles production.

Text input

We'll start at the beginning, and in the beginning is the word. Someone has to write the text.

It is very common today for even the stubborn, diehard writer to use a computer, and to send his or her material to the publisher on floppy disk. It is also quite common for a writer to send material over the phone. And although it is still common for a raw manuscript to be pounded out on a mechanical typewriter, few publishers encourage such primitive use of technology.

What kind of software does the average writer use to "write?" Typically, a word processor which has at least the ability to help check spelling. In addition, some writers like to have an electronic thesaurus available, which can instantly look up synonyms.

A good word processor can do lots of tricks, like put hidden "markers" in the file, generate an index or table of contents, and more. But just as important is the screen presentation itself. Are the words easy to read on the screen? Can the writer move quickly from one part of the job to another? Is the search-and-replace function of the word processor easy and fast? What about that page makeup software, like Ventura Publisher and Aldus Pagemaker? Why doesn't the writer just use one of them, so he or she can see "exactly" what the job will look like?

There are dozens of reasons, some of which are spelled out by the software publishers themselves. But generally the reasons can be lumped into two categories: Speed and ability. The word processor has more speed and more of the abilities that the writer will make use of, including those just mentioned (thesaurus, search-and-replace, legible screen). In addition, it is not too often that the writer is generating "final" material. It will quite probably be read, edited, or slightly modified by another editor or writer. The typographic qualities of the job are probably not yet finalized. But the bottom line is the obvious one: The writer is merely putting together words, not pages, and not galleys. He is not, at this stage, performing hyphenation or justification, or dropping initials, or doing copy run-arounds. He's just writing, and the tool of choice, every time, is a word processor — not a program that makes pages.

Keystrokes

If the writer does not submit material electronically, the publisher must have it keyboarded, or keystroked.

Now you might think that the "obvious" way to get that done is to tell an employee to do it. But that makes an assumption: How do we know whether this publisher even owns a computer or typewriter? Sure, all of the DTP people have computers. But not all professional publishers have them. I just visited a firm in Florida that doesn't have a single computer, or a single typist on the staff. They publish a very successful quarterly journal, and run four companion trade shows. The publisher would rather golf than type, so he does.

So, the publisher first decides how to go about getting the manuscript typed (if necessary). Once material is typed, it might be edited on paper, or edited on a computer screen, but it *will* quite probably be edited. (There are exceptions to that rule, too. Some of the "professional" publishers out there print unedited trash, and pass it off as "stories" about their particular industry.)

In most cases, the job will not be seen next as a "page." Rather, it will be viewed as a "galley." This is usually done because still more changes might be made at the galley stage by an editor. Things that might be modified include hyphenation, the killing of widows (lone words on a line), and the length of the piece itself.

Can DTP systems be used to generate galleys? Certainly. The galleys might appear three to a page, or the operator might generate them one galley to a sheet of paper. So the question is not the hardware or the software. The question is, what does the typical publisher prefer to see at this point, pages or galleys?

Most want galleys. (I'm not saying what they *should* do, mind you. Just what *most* do.) Those galleys might be used to create paper layouts or "thumbnail sketches." Or they might be marked up and returned, with a request for a second set of galleys.

At some point, the publisher decides it is time to design the pages (or do the layouts). Most layouts, as of today, are done on paper. The galleys might be copied on an office copier and taped to position. Or the layouts might be less specific than that, calling for 6 inches of copy here, 9 inches there, etc.

Why do most publishers do layouts on paper? One reason is that most publishers are not using integrated software, which is what all DTP software actually is. That's not to say they won't change their style over the next few years. But for now, the most common way to design or lay out a publication is with a pencil or copies of the galleys.

Other things normally decided upon during the layout stage are the photos to be used, their positions and sizes, and whether they will be used in color or not.

With the layouts complete, the page is ready for "assembly." It might be run one more time as galleys, and then cut and pasted with wax or glue. Or it might be assembled on a huge composition system. Or it might be run on a small DTP system.

When the page is built, we now have (regardless of whether we used DTP or not) the pasteup boards, or art boards, or mechanicals, or any other of the buzz-names. We have typesetting, rules, borders, and simple line artwork. We do not have photos or color graphics on the page just yet, regardless of which common system we're using.

Now bear with me while I digress for a moment. Aren't some publications produced on multi-million dollar, full-page, full-color composition systems? The answer is yes. All of the weekly news magazines are. But few of the monthly magazines are. And of the 12,000 different magazine titles in the country, only a fraction of a percent would be produced on such systems. Of the tens of thousands of catalogs produced in the U.S., only that same fraction of a percent would be produced entirely by electronic means. Virtually no books would be published that way, as a percentage of the total numbers of books published each year. Why so few magazines, catalogs, and books done with the fancy color page-makeup machines? Cost, speed, and data storage. Or to put it another way, that technology is not practical for the typical publication.

So, what we probably have at this stage is the text, borders, rules, boxes, panels, and other ultra-simple shapes. Now, using "typical" technology (not the ultra-high-cost stuff mentioned in the preceding digression), how would we add a black and white photo? With a scanner? Using DTP or another electronic method?

Not normally. We would typically have a black-and-white photo shot on a lithographic camera, directly to litho film. There would be no electronic storage of the photo. Rather, it would be converted to a film negative with a dot pattern representing light and dark areas of the photo. That film negative would be "stripped" (or, more precisely, taped) into position relative to other material on that page, and the page would be stripped relative to other pages in the publication. Shooting the photo to film is called shooting a halftone, and it typically costs from $5.00 to $10.00 per photo.

As an alternative, we might choose to have the photo scanned. This would be performed on a color or black-and-white scanning machine, but would be output only to litho film. We would not store the material electronically. So what's all this stuff you read about DTP and scanning photos? In the real world it doesn't exist. For many years in this business of publishing, we have had the ability to scan, store, retrieve, manipulate, and electronically position photos in black and white or color. But even the smallest black-and-white photo would consume 100,000 to a million bytes of precious computer storage. A tiny color photo might require five million bytes of magnetic storage. The computer console and working environment required to view the page might cost several hundred thousand dollars; the entire installation several million.

So in the real, workaday world of publishing, we have black and white photos rather primitively converted to film images, which are physically positioned by a human being called a stripper. What about color?

Again, although the technology is there, it isn't used to do everything it could possibly do. Color photos are scanned on an electronic machine, and are converted again to screened film, one piece of film for each of the four primary printing colors.

Low-cost scanners

Why don't professional publishers make use of the new low-cost scanning devices available to DTP users? As mentioned in the opening chapter, not even staunch DTP advocates use cheap scanners. The reasons are several:
- Too much electronic storage required; too expensive to purchase.
- Quality well beneath conventional publishing standards.
- Relative difficulty in long-term retrieval.

There's an easier way to say that. It ain't broke, so we ain't fixing it. For the time being, the excellent controls and moderate costs available in conventional electronic scanning (directly to film) offer a practical, efficient way into print.

That's not to say you cannot mingle the old with the new, and DTP with conventional means. For example, my firm and many others do not always run "paper" typesetting output on our high-quality equipment. If the firm we're dealing with uses DTP and would prefer to stick with a few operating groundrules, we can skip the phototypesetting paper, and output directly to litho film. That saves the cost of the paper, which is not cheap. It also saves a complete step in the production cycle — the task of shooting the phototypesetting output on a camera in order to convert it to film.

The advertising mix

There's another reason many publishers aren't holding their breath in hopes of becoming fully electronic. Take a look at the average magazine, newspaper, or catalog. Guess which method is most commonly used to transport a complete page?

Answer: Film negatives (or, in some cases, film positives). Final film negatives cannot be taken "backwards" with any current success. That means, they must be positioned by our friendly stripper. And that means, virtually all of the 12,000 magazines in this country will not be "totally" electronic in the forseeable future. There is no growing trend for advertisers to send a bulky, 10-pound magnetic tape to a magazine, instead of sending four cheap pieces of film.

That brings up the reality of film, and the reason it is used for halftones, color photos, and virtually everything else. It is cheap. That's right: A dollar's worth of film can hold five megabytes of electronic information, and then some. In today's dollars, a megabyte costs over $500. So our buck in film buys the equivalent of $2,500 of computer memory. That's just to make a point, of course. You wouldn't attempt to store an entire catalog in memory; you would store it on magnetic tape, or on a disk. But the fact is, you'd be dealing with many gigabytes of information for a typical catalog, magazine, or book. Using conventional technology and DTP, there's no way you can store and easily manipulate the average publication.

Given that the typical publisher prefers to store "completed" jobs for up to several years, you can see that for now, film is an absolute requirement — at least until electronic storage becomes virtually free, and we can instantly access much larger storage devices than a tiny 60 megabyte hard disk.

Changes to come

Let's dream a bit. What if DTP had access to unlimited gigabyte disks for storage? What if the developments in low-cost color scanners, using TV-camera technology instead of laser-scanning technolgy, become highly practical? What if most advertisers choose to send digital color and text on a CD ROM? What if the typical office computer has direct access to 32 megabytes of memory, and memory becomes inexpensive? What if cheap, ultra-fast output becomes available?

All of that appears to be happening. And when it does, professional service houses (and consequently, publishers) will be the first ones to intelligently transition to the new tools. The industry has always responded positively to good ideas in the past, and shows no signs of suddenly becoming technosenile. But until the equipment has the power to handle life in the real world, we will be using cameras and scanners, and taping pieces of film to mylar, and pretty much doing things the way we've been doing them for the past few years — but in some cases, with the certain added ability and speed offered by DTP typesetting and pagination systems.

But for now, the true publishing professional first needs a knowledge of conventional means. He or she can benefit from DTP by adding some DTP power to those conventional methods. And as each area of conventional technology is outperformed by DTP or any other hardware or software, the evolution will continue.

The professional certainly doesn't change everything, all at once, with the naive belief that technology moves so fast that (1) the typesetting business, (2) the color separation business, (3) the lithographic stripping business, (4) the proofing business, (5) the advertising business, and (6) the business of publishing itself, would change completely overnight. We're pros, we've seen change before, we continually adapt to it, we use it when it works, and over a period of every 50 years or so, we do see a complete revolution. It didn't start with DTP and it won't, by any means, end with it. On the contrary, the last major revolution started with offset lithography, and that revolution continues.

The one-shop assumption

Given the above, you might think that "real" publishers tend to think things through, and tend to take their time when tossing out a complete system or technological tool. Of course. That only makes sense.

These same publishers would rarely make the mistake being made so frequently today by "new" publishers — or, DTP users gone public.

By now, most printers have gotten short phone calls from potential clients. They go like this:

"Hello, I need a price for printing my magazine, but I need to know if you do high-quality desktop publishing output."

"Ah, no, but I'm sure we could arrange that for you."

"No. I need a printer who does desktop publishing. Thank you. Click."

And double click.

Oh you do, do you? You call a printer to discuss DTP. Do you then call a Mac owner to get advice on printing? What's the matter with these people?

Nothing. They are merely ignorant. They are newcomers to an old, established business — the business of printing. They feel that once they have their page perfected on their screen and their laser proofing machine, that it should now be "printing." So they call printers.

In the quick-print field, such logic sometimes works. A small minority of quick printers have added DTP systems — typically, just low-end, low-resolution systems. But they add such systems for reasons quite different than the publisher. They deliberately add DTP as a low-end typesetting department for low-quality, fast-turnaround work.

But in the business of publication, catalog, and book printing it might be silly to think that printers would hop into the DTP field. It took these same printers decades to shut down their hot-metal typesetting departments, and today, most major printers are either out of — or getting out of — page makeup technology. As a printer shuts down the art department and closes the door on typesetting, does it make sense that he tosses in an L-300, and a supplemental art department, and a small typesetting front end, just to attract the business of the publisher who has not even arranged for outputting his product to film or paper? Not hardly.

In fact, it is just as typical for a printer to say, "We'd prefer you ship us film negatives. That's the only way we can give you a hard, predictable price and delivery schedule."

And that's true. The real uncertainty on any printing invoice will rotate around the things that can't be predicted: Corrections, alterations, the number of color photos, and everything else that must be locked in before final film is sent to the press.

Of course, "real" publishers don't assume that just because they need a different device to output their typesetting, their printer will purchase it. Rather, today's publisher is aware that there is tremendous change in the hardware of typesetting and page output, and that anyone who sticks $100,000 into that field is rolling the dice.

Summary

- Most professional publishing firms do not use DTP, but many are transitioning to it at some level and for only certain tasks. The professional use of DTP is often limited to text, rules, and panels.
- Photos and artwork are generally handled by conventional methods. A small handful of publishers are experimenting with color illustrations and separations using DTP technology. Generally speaking, the technology is still experimental or too impractical for the typical publisher.
- Virtually all publishers in the country use conventional means to print B-W and color photos, including those who publish magazines on how to publish using DTP.

Chapter 5:

What Does It Really Cost?

In an article in *Successful Magazine Publishing,* a DTP advocate claimed that a complete "publishing system" could be purchased for $6,000, and that it would eliminate all typesetting, artwork and film preparation charges. Another trade magazine (for small printers) stated that the "complete" system might cost $12,000, but warned that only medium-quality output would be available.

Which article was right? Neither. They describe only the hardware required for manipulating text and generating low-resolution proofs (at most). And although the author who used the $6,000 figure claimed that such a system could easily produce a monthly, 128-page magazine, the truth is possibly $244,000 away.

Separating goals from hype

Hardware manufacturers have a single goal: selling hardware. So it makes little sense to ask someone who sells DTP hardware what he or she would recommend. Rather, you want to start with needs and goals. And they must be your own. We'll start with a customer I interviewed in Florida.

"Where are your computers?" I asked.

"We don't have any, and we don't want any. Here's what I do. I'll give you a story and some pictures, and tell you what the headline is, and how big to make the photos. You'll tell me about how many pages it will fill, and later you show me a proof."

Try selling a system to this guy!

Next, a good customer of mine in Detroit.

"Well, all we really want to do is see line endings on the screen and generate something on paper so we can do a layout. We need to get our galleys turned around faster. We don't want to learn too much about the technical end. Laser proofs would be nice, but any other way to get the galley would be fine, too."

I asked, "Do you want to generate the entire publication on the screen? Do you plan to put in all the rules and photos?"

"Maybe later," he said. "But for now, we just want to solve the problem of getting galley proofs faster than we have been. The way it is now, it takes two or three days from the time we release the material to the typesetter until we get the galleys for layout purposes. If we could just get the galley faster, we'd be happy."

So I asked a few more questions. I needed to know how many persons would be working on the computer, how much material would be processed, what the budget might be, whether they required a reasonably accurate proof or could live with simulated typefaces, and so forth.

The answers indicated that one person at the firm would be responsible for "getting the galleys" out of the system, and that the quality of the proofs should be good enough for proofreading, layout, and a general feel for the finished product. They would not be attempting to generate artwork, they did not want to produce final, high-quality paper or film, and they expected that a professional firm would finish the job on a more elaborate system.

That firm could get by with "minimal" equipment: $5,000 for a computer and high-quality monitor, and maybe $3,500 for a laser proofing device. They would not have the ability to incorporate photos or complex graphics, but then, they knew what they wanted anyhow: the ability to quickly generate a galley so they could design their publication and do proofreading.

High-quality output

So were those writers correct? Does this publisher have a DTP system for less than $10,000? Hardly. The publisher has the ability to manipulate text, boxes, and rules on the screen, and to generate a cheap, low-resolution proof. But with this setup, he couldn't possibly eliminate all of his typesetting costs. Nor would he be eliminating any significant film preparation costs.

In order to get high-quality output, the material must be run on a laser device costing from $30,000 to $75,000. And the $75,000 machine is the one most commonly running at a firm which offers laser output services, because it is a reasonably fast machine.

What about art and photos? They, and everything else must be done either conventionally, or by a far more powerful and expensive system. That includes converting black and white photos to screened film, and performing color separations on the color photos. (While the *concept* of doing color separation work on a small computer is there, as of early 1989 it is not practical in most cases.)

Back to the question. What does our publisher get for $10,000 or less? Is it a complete system? No. Even if the low-resolution output is acceptable, the system cannot handle photos or artwork, and cannot produce film output. It can merely generate low-quality paper output, which might be fine for quick brochures or other quick-print type material.

If that publisher wants any kind of quality — for example, the level of quality in a magazine — then the system is nothing more than a typesetting and layout front end. And there is nothing wrong with that: Only 10 years ago, a system which could set type and manipulate in on the screen would have cost several hundred thousand dollars.

The other extreme

Now let's add enough equipment to "eliminate typesetting, artwork, and film preparation" as our $6,000 advocate said we could. We'll build only a basic system with no redundancy, so if you want backup, double the numbers.

We'll start with that basic computer and laser proofing device for $8,500. But in order to discuss doing "film preparation," we must immediately add a laser output device capable of producing film. While there are devices available for $40,000, they are not the "big-name" machines. If we merely decide to buy what the average professional would buy, we'll spend $75,000 on the device.

To that device we must add typefaces. We'll purchase 100 of them at $50 each, giving us a small type library. And making us another $5,000 poorer.

Now the kicker. That author claimed that her little system could eliminate the film preparation charges for her magazine. What would we need to be able to convert black and white photos so we could see them, manipulate them on screen, and output them to film? To generate them at magazine-quality level, we'd spend a hundred thousand dollars. That's right: A hundred grand. And that is only for a top notch black-and-white scanner.

What if you don't need magazine-level quality? You could drop down to a $2,500 scanner. But remember, at the time of this writing, those magazines which specialize in using (and preaching about) DTP systems do not use either variety of scanner — low cost or high. They have their black and white photos shot on a conventional lithographic camera, and their color photos separated on a lithographic scanner.

Does it seem odd that a magazine which praises DTP and has access to hundreds of thousands of dollars of equipment would REVIEW black and white scanners, but not USE them? Sure. They publish a conventional-quality magazine, not a low-resolution, low-cost rag. Although they can hide many of the problems they have, they can't hide low-quality photo reproduction. So they use and admit to "conventional" means.

If you were to take this system to a color level, you'd go into shock. There you'd spend $500,000 or more for a scanner, plus the interface to connect it to your little desktop system.

The bottom line? It is not practical, but here it is. In order to eliminate all typesetting and film preparation costs for a typical magazine, you'd spend $100,000 plus on the DTP computer and laser output device, and $100,000 for a quality black-and-white scanner. To add color, you'd be talking several million dollars in 1989 dollars.

In other words, it is virtually impossible to say that DTP can eliminate "all" of this cost and "all" of that cost. Certainly, the concept of producing "all" of your own film and saving "all" preparation costs is outrageous.

A more logical DTP approach

Chances are you can spend more than $6,000, but don't want to spend $2 million. What are the logical middle positions?

Let's return to the magazine example. Can you spend less than $10,000 but still produce a monthly 128-page magazine? Not really. Consider my friends in Florida.

I visited with them in early 1989. They produce a 112-page bimonthly magazine, along with books, brochures, and other related material. They have only one computer workstation that does typesetting and page makeup. They own and use both Aldus Pagemaker and Ventura Publisher.

And, they "produce" their entire magazine on the system. Or do they?

Well, they have four other computers in the shop. Much of their editorial material is keyboarded on those computers. Still more of it is sent to them on disk by their contributors. Editorial functions are not performed on the DTP computer — that would tie it up too much.

Still, with a single computer and a laser proofer, they do all of the magazine's typesetting — sort of. They do all of the hyphenation, justification, proofing, layout, editing, and alterations right on the screen. They run proofs on the laser device. But then they send their disks to a typesetting firm to be run as high-quality paper output on a Linotronic L-300.

They take that paper output and paste it onto conventional pasteup boards, and to that they add photostats. They might also put "flaps" on the boards, along with office-copier enlargements or reductions showing how photos are to be positioned and cropped.

In the frequent case that an advertisement has been supplied as a film negative, they put a paper copy of the ad in position. And if a page needs a photo in color, they indicate its ultimate size, and instruct their film preparation house to do a color separation.

Is it desktop?

Why does this publisher limit the company's use of DTP to mostly text and layout? Why not take it all the way? To this publisher, the answer is quite obvious. He is a professional magazine publisher who saw something that made his job easier and potentially more cost effective. So he decided to implement that "something." But he didn't buy one of everything. Certain equipment, including these examples, had too many problems or limitations.

- **B-W scanner.** Would not make things easier for his company. Would not produce the quality he was currently getting. Would be reasonably cost effective if quality was not required, but not cost effective at all if quality were to be maintained.
- **High-resolution output.** He had not owned or operated typesetting hardware in the past because he preferred not to invest into even the $40,000 conventional systems. The fact that systems were now laser-based did not change his mind. The typical $80,000 investment had already been made by the typesetting firm he had used for years. They had more than enough open time to take care of his needs in a timely manner at a reasonable page cost (in fact, a cost far less than he previously had been paying).
- **Color scanner.** Don't be silly.
- **More workstations.** The schedule is bimonthly, and he has only one art director. The editors do not necessarily need to work "on screen." The sequence is to produce galleys for proofreading, then page proofs of "final" layout and design.

A larger system

Another publishing firm I toured (located in Milwaukee) produced three monthly magazines. As you would expect, they had more equipment than the Florida operation.

They had eleven Macintoshes all hooked to a central file server. They had a single laser proofing device. Three of the workstations were equipped with the more costly 19-inch monitors ($2,000 to $5,000). You might roughly estimate that they spentd $60,000 or so on the setup. But still no scanner, and still, no high-resolution output. Why?

Their goal in installing the entire system was to save money on typesetting and pagination. It was already assumed that all of the editors would need to be working on some type of computer, even if it were merely for word processing. So they purchased what they felt was the minimal equipment to put their entire editorial and art staff on computers, giving them the ability to design the basic page. Like all operations I toured, adding photos of any sort to the electronic page was out of the question.

A bridge system

One very interesting installation I'm familiar with is operated by a publisher in Chicago. This firm puts out several publications, and their equipment consists of a Macintosh SE, a 60 megabyte hard disk drive, a Laserwriter, and a $5,000 color monitor.

The interesting thing about this firm is that they don't have an art director on the staff, they don't do their own final output, and they ultimately send color-broken negatives to their film preparation house. So who does the DTP design and layout? A free-lancer.

All of their design and page makeup work, and all of the hyphenation and justification, are farmed out to a DTP free-lance art director who uses a similar installation to design and proof the publications. At the publishing office itself, the hardware is primarily there to view the art director's output, to transmit the material to a service bureau which runs the high-resolution negatives, and to keep things coordinated. You might call the entire computer setup a publishing "bridge," which connects the designers, writers, and service bureau.

While this is a unique setup, it does the job for this firm. They have approximately $16,000 in hardware, lots of software, but no art director, designer, or typesetters on the staff. True, they pay for those services on a fee basis, but they are pleased. They have a manageable staff, and the ability to move their work to other vendors or free-lancers at will.

The net result

So. Is it true that you can purchase a "complete" system for $6,000 to $12,000? If your definition of "complete" is that you need only a certain amount of ability and control, then yes. But will it eliminate all typesetting, art, layout, design, and film preparation costs? Not by a long shot.

It will primarily reduce the outside *labor costs* associated with conventional typesetting and page assembly. It is not likely to eliminate design costs, unless you decide to use the same page design over and over. And likewise, you are not obligated to purchase a complete DTP system in order to reduce labor costs, pick up speed, and so on. As mentioned in the last example, DTP services — including design and proofs — can be purchased from a free-lancer, a typesetting firm, a film preparation house, or anyone else you find who has expertise in design, along with the required equipment.

And that identifies one of the more significant fallacies perpetrated by the DTP sales force. Think about it: In those cases where DTP makes a job easier, faster, and better, won't those who already specialize in typesetting and page design use the DTP tools? Sure. Can you still purchase their services? Sure. Will it cost less than it used to? In this competitive business, the answer, again, is sure.

Or, as in the past, any publisher who wants to purchase typesetting equipment, litho cameras, processors, or even printing presses, is free to do so. Some publishers want to do it all, and some want to do as little as possible. But don't be tricked into thinking you "must" purchase a department full of equipment in order to take advantage of new technology. You never had to before, and you don't have to now. You will always have the option of doing it in house, but likewise, you can always purchase those services outside, from a conventional firm, or a new DTP specialist.

Summary

- DTP workstations can be installed for $6,000 to $10,000, and that might include a proofing device.
- It is highly unlikely that you would want a "complete" DTP system. With today's technology, that would require from $500,000 to $2 million in order to deliver most of the claims made about DTP.
- You can enter the DTP field on an experimental or tentative basis for less than $10,000, and build your department up if required and desired.

Chapter 6:

I Don't Know Art But...

Nearly 15 years ago, some of the so-called womens' magazines began to graphically regurgitate at their readers. But, as is so often the case with vile fashion, it was legitimized by gaining buzzword status. It was called *new wave* graphic design, and it coincided with other vapid, tasteless things called new wave in the middle to late 1970s.

How was new wave different from "normal" design? It was deliberately tasteless and senseless.

For example, instead of using two colors to create harmony, the new wave graphic artist would attempt to use two colors which clashed horribly, say, shocking pink with green. If they were sufficiently obnoxious, they qualified as new wave. How obnoxious did they have to be? Well, it was sort of like this: If there was any shadow of doubt in your mind that the designer *accidentally* made the page look horrible, instead of *deliberately* making it look horrible, it was not good new wave. With tasteless, there had to be no doubt whatsoever.

Soon, the new wave got bigger. It began to encompass any stupid, tasteless use of typography or design whose sole and obvious purpose was to get attention.

By the mid 80's, you no longer heard the term new wave in the graphic design circles. But it left its mark, for sure! Virtually every otherwise respectable magazine, catalog, and even newspaper, has been contaminated at some level by new wave radioactivity. (We still don't know the half-life of this stuff.)

How can such contamination be identified? With a simple test: Page through a magazine or other publication, and try to figure out *why* a particular thing was done. If, after beating your head against the wall, you can only say "I guess it was done to get attention," you're looking at what used to be called new wave, but what is now just bad design. Design for its own sake. Or in some cases (please, if you have a weak stomach, skip to the next paragraph right now!), deliberately disgusting, attention getting, graphic vomit.

So, you might ask. What does all of this talk of poor design, of senseless graphics, of insulting the reader for the sake of bad design in the name of good design . . . what, you might wonder, does all of this have to do with DTP?

It is an odd relationship, but here it is. DTP users tend to read magazines which focus on DTP. There are, at this time, several magazines devoted to DTP. In those magazines, the DTP user reads about typesetting, design, layout, and artwork. (Never mind that they rarely, if *ever*, discuss the reality of actually publishing. Instead they talk about typesetting, but *call* it publishing.)

And, sad to say, the DTP magazines use the most outrageous, senseless, insulting, tasteless graphic design in print today — outside that produced by their readers, of course, who are imitating them so senselessly that the results are even more outrageous.

I have a degree in design. No kidding — even us writers must have a useless degree in something, and mine is technically in Fine Arts (minus approximately 8 credits; they closed the school). Major area of focus: Graphic design. For four years, I studied how to make things look "good"in print — to give a page balance, sense, meaning. Relevance, even! (Another dead word.)

So, see if you can figure out if the following is a graphic joke that I made up, or whether it's real.

Get a sheet of 8-1/2 by 11 inch white paper, a pencil, and a ruler. I'm going to help you design a magazine page. It will be the table of contents page. Ready?

We'll start at the top of the page. Three inches from the left side, draw a rectangle which is 1/4 inch thick, 1-1/2 inches wide, and which has one side (the long side) flush with the top of the paper. What will it mean? I don't want to say yet. But color it green, if you have a marker. Why green? Because.

Now I want you to draw a very thin rule. Start about 2 inches down from the top, and make it about 6 inches long. Then skip a half inch. Then continue with it for another 2 inches. Now you should have a vertical rule with an empty space in it, right?

Okay then, starting at the left edge of the paper, just opposite that hole, write the alphabet in lower case letters about 3/8 inches tall. But not the whole alphabet. Start somewhere in the middle — like, with the letter *L*. Draw the "l" so that it is half on the page and half off the page. Make the alphabet end about 4 inches across the page.

While we're talking about alphabets, let's add another whole alphabet, but this time in all capital italic letters. To add this one, turn your page sideways. Now, at the lower left of the sheet, about a quarter inch from the bottom, and a half inch from the left, write the whole alphabet in letters about 1/8 inch tall. Make it about 4 inches long altogether, and turn the page back to normal.

Now you should have one alphabet running vertically, in all caps, in little letters located in the upper left (what we call the gutter, if this is a right-hand page), and about a half of an alphabet toward the bottom of the page running in from the left, to nearly half way across the page. And you have a rectangle up at the top. In green. Guess what the rectangle is for.

About 2 inches directly below the rectangle, put in the number 42, about a quarter inch tall. Then move over to the right. When you get to the part of the page that is not beneath the rectangle, write in tiny, bold letters (maybe 1/16 inch tall), HOW TO DESIGN.

Get it? That rectangle up there which is apparently not doing anything but looking green is actually saying, "I'm just as wide as an arbitrary indent you will find later on in this page. However, certain elements of the page will deliberately not honor the arbitrary indent, for added interest and visual excitement."

I Don't Know Art But . . .

And what about those alphabets? Were they deliberately dropped onto the page as if by accident? Yessir. That's what makes this kind of design non-dis-intentional, as Pogo might say. We deliberately put things where the reader doesn't expect them, where he or she can't possibly figure out a purpose or reason. When the reader is truly shocked, we have succeeded. But like new wave: If that reader wonders for a moment whether it is in *good taste* to put an alphabet, in caps, in italics, on its side, vertically in the gutter, then we have failed. He should not have *wondered* about good taste.

So, you get the idea. While we could continue until you had a complete table of contents in front of you, there's an easier way. It was a true example. Subscribe to the DTP magazines, and you will have proof positive.

Am I kidding?

I wish. That table of contents page we were describing touches upon only a handful of the senseless graphic insults in what might be the world's most popular and respected DTP magazine. Rather than try to teach their readers that graphic temperance is an insurance policy for the novice, they preach — and print — shock graphics.

As I read in one article in that magazine, "Shock your audience by . . . placing the graphic in an unusual position on the page. Run it smaller than you might . . . getting people's attention by surprising them works."

In other words, tastelessness works. Garbage works. Anything the reader doesn't expect, works. And for this I studied for four years in college?

You can imagine the trash this advice generates. The newcomer to DTP (typically, some dude who just bought a Mac and wants to start publishin' fast) reads that the secret to communication is drop your pants, flash the reader, get his attention by hitting him with a two by four. If we took the same approach with editorial, we might say, use dirty words, misquote the Bible, say nice things about terrorists. Just get that reader's attention. Shock him.

Obviously something's missing in this picture. What?

Purpose. Instead of using and preaching purpose in design, purpose in writing, even (for heaven's sake) purpose in publishing, we see deliberate lack of purpose. By redefining it as shock graphics, we give it a name, and the closer that name becomes to a buzzword, the more our purposelessness becomes legitimized, until — like new wave — it actually becomes accepted as good design.

So you have two ways to generate bad design. Make something look bad on purpose, and take credit for it, or make it look bad by accident, and be ashamed of it. You can see why the DTP publishers take the first approach. It's makes them look better with no additional effort. They just have to maintain that consistent lack-of-purpose look and feel.

Here are a few sure fire pointers for making your reader wonder what kind of drugs you were taking when you designed your publication. If he can find purpose in each of these, he takes the same drugs.

I Don't Know Art But...

Design tips from DTP magazines

In paging through my collection of magazines designed by DTP "professionals," I've collected a series of tips to help you get started on the road to DTP graphics.

- **Vertical rules between columns.** Everyone thinks they should be solid. Make yours out of dots. A row of vertical dots. Purple dots.
- **Paragraph indents.** Too many people indent just a little bit. Indent your paragraphs half way across the column.
- **Novel paragraph indents.** Who says the first part of a paragraph has to start further in? Make it start further out. And put the first word in an orange rectangle.
- **Cap one word of a head.** For the heck of it, run the first word of a headline in cap letters, and the second word in uppers and lowers. The reader will go crazy trying to figure out whether you meant that the first word was more important.
- **Make the columns unequal in length.** This not only makes the reader wonder if you meant to do it, but it makes designing the page a lot easier, too.
- **Use surprise rectangles.** Just put some on the page where you think they'll surprise the reader. Occasionally, make a rectangle 1-1/2 inches thick and a foot long. Put it at the top of a two page spread. It's a real surprise.
- **S p a c e O u t T h e B y l i n e s.** Just put space between every letter of the names of authors, like that. It'll drive people nuts.
- **Use clip-art.** But only in a way the reader knows that you know that it *is* clip art, and that you are not using it

because it is *good,* but becauseit is *bad*. Be careful with this one. It can be misinterpreted.
- **Throw an alphabet in somewhere.** Admittedly, this makes insulting, surprising sense mostly if you are publishing a DTP magazine, but what the heck. It might be even *more* of a surprise in a medical journal.
- **Underline everything.** This is particularly shocking and effective when it makes, for example, an advertisement very hard to read. Or use it to trick the reader into thinking that there are three headlines on the page, when in fact there is only one, underlined.
- **Put some triangles on the page.** Like surprise rectangles, the reader will wonder what these are for.
- **Arbitrary rules.** Stodgy old-timers use rules to separate things. But you can use them for no reason. For a special treat, join a thick and thin rule at a right angle, and put the result on the page where the reader doesn't expect it. In red.
- **Use caps with small caps.** But don't do this predictably. Do it every other time you feel like it, plus once in a while when you don't.
- **Use old-fashioned typefaces.** In the mid 50's we had people using sans-serif condensed faces for just about everything. By using them now, you'll insult the designers with a sense of history, and shock the novices. Two birds with one stone.
- **Give things two names.** Like, *Desktop Publishing PUBLISH!*, or *REVIEW Portfolio*. Let the reader figure out which is the real name. (Note the use of two techniques in the latter example: meaningless capitalization with a two-name title. *Very* effective.)

- **Be inconsistent.** Remember, shock value is where it's at. If you can afford it, re-design or, better still, de-design your publication every year. Or even every issue.

Am I being too hard on the DTP journals? Goodness no. Pick one up. Page through it. Think about shock value, about purpose. Think about the four years I wasted learning to make ink make sense. Then write those folks a letter, and tell them how you feel. Whether created by accident or deliberately for the sake of shock, bad design is bad design, and enough is enough.

Summary

- DTP advocates often have an aggressive, maverick graphic style, which is not necessarily in good taste, and which may result either from lack of training or an earnest desire to look different.
- Designing a quality piece does not require that you shock or surprise your audience into looking at what you have. That's called flashing, and it's illegal in most states.
- You will learn more about design by studying the average newsstand than by reading a magazine which uses shock graphics in an attempt to teach design.

Chapter 7:

DTP and Other Drugs

Some years ago, I saw a demonstration of a software package that could justify text, pour the text into pages, put photos and art on the page, output a cheap laser proof, and drive any typesetting device, conventional or imagesetter.

It also allowed the untrained user to create screen fonts, generate special logos or designs, load typeface widths from any typesetting system, do extremely complex runarounds, batch-produce magazines and books, and more.

Yes sir. This little baby could do it all. So I became a dealer. (And as I relate DTP to a drug addiction, you can determine the morality of that occupation.) But there was one minor problem that set me apart from other dealers for the firm. I wanted to install the product, use it, and then sell it. I figured, what better way to sell it than to show it in action?

Is it hard to believe that I was the *only* dealer for this firm who wanted to install and use the product? I think so. But that was the fact.

So I sat myself down, read the instruction manual, and installed the software. But I soon began to stumble. I found little bugs that would puzzle me for hours. I would call the company and ask for help, but more often than not, they would record my comments, and promise to "look into it." But I was determined to get this thing up and running.

My typical "attack" would be composed of 60 hours in a given week, working my way through font mapping, width loading, tag writing, and general customization for my testbed newsletter — a twelve pager. But still, the bugs. Always another bug. I was beginning to get frustrated when, finally, the company called the entire sales force to headquarters. They were going to distribute the new, debugged version of the program. I was relieved. I bought a ticket, hopped on a plane, and soon found myself in a room with 50 other dealers, all apparently as desperate as I. We needed something that worked.

Well, it wasn't quite ready yet, so the company officers entertained us by telling us what it would do when they finally released it. But many in that room were vocal. Upset. They accused a company officer of not paying attention to our problems. He vehemently stated that he was doing everything he could, and that they had already fixed 500 reported problems, or bugs. (What? I only reported 27! No kidding. This officer more or less *bragged* that they had fixed over 500 bugs that had been reported . . . *after* they had sold 400 copies of the program.) Then they sent us home.

I shared a cab with another dealer as we headed for the airport. During the ride, he stated in clear, raw terms, what he wanted the company to do with its next release. He quit, right then and there, and decided to represent another firm. (I lost respect for him only when he told me its name — another "super duper" product designed to reinvent the process of typesetting while calling it publishing.)

Several weeks later, I received The New Version. How excited I was. Finally, all of those annoying bugs and problems. Finally, I'd be able to do an honest demonstration that would not embarrass me. And finally, I'd be able to do a prototype newsletter. A little 12 pager.

By now I had over 750 hours invested in learning and installing the software. All of my editorial was written and on disk, so all I had to do was "pour" the text into the pages. Ah, but not so fast. We still had *bugs*.

It took me 60 hours to lay that text into pages. No photos, no art. Just text. Sixty hours. I was suicidal.

I called the company with my recommendations and complaints. At about the same time, I began to receive weekly reports from the company, marked "strictly confidential," and always on the topics of "fixes and workarounds." It was the weekly bug report.

Finally, I sent them a letter releasing my territory, and telling them that I was not merely disappointed, but disgusted with what they had done. Here they were, selling some of the most expensive software on the market, claiming it could do more than any other software available, and the $%!@ thing didn't even *work!* Had they no morals? No ethics? No shame? I don't know. I know they had a lot of customers' money, though.

Withdrawal

For the next two years, I maintained my distance from DTP. I had learned a lot by studying the guts of the stuff I was planning to sell. I took it apart, piece by piece, and became intimately familiar with the components that a DTP system would have to organize. But after publicly announcing that I was dropping the product because it did not work, I wanted to be very careful before I jumped back on the DTP bandwagon.

Meanwhile, one of the company's top salesmen left. He decided to join a typesetting firm, where he and another expert would install the same software that I had said would not run. Believe it or not, he and another person *with expert knowledge* of the software each spent 500 hours on the project. That's 1,000 labor hours. And they knew what they were doing. No wonder I couldn't make it run. They never did, either. Not as advertised, anyhow.

After saying a few thousand times, *I told you so,* I quieted down. I spent time with customers, interviewing clients who were using, or planning to use, DTP. I stayed as current as I could on new software and developing DTP abilities.

Meanwhile, the company I had represented announced that they were introducing their "New, New" software. They were abandoning support of the earlier release (meaning: frozen bugs). They were holding dealer meetings, and discussing the strategy of convincing former customers to "upgrade," and at a handsome fee. Imagine. After these poor customers suffered for several years with software that never worked, the company salesman pops by and, instead of a free upgrade, tells you that the only solution is to purchase the new product.

I was also becoming quite critical of DTP as a whole. Much of my writing for the trade magazines took on a negative twist. I made fun of people who tried to scan photos, import graphics, and "drive any typesetting device in the world." I still do.

I made fun of professionals who were content to look at a picture of an hourglass on their computer screen, never wondering why their computer had only one processing chip which had to perform all computing tasks (like refreshing the screen with that little clock), which made one of the world's fastest chips manage so many chores at once that it ended up running one of the world's slowest desktop computers. Yeah, I guess I still make fun of those people, too.

I suppose I made fun of anyone who did not have a technical understanding of what they wanted computers, and DTP in particular, to deliver. And I still do.

But after several years and several evolutions of Aldus Pagemaker and Ventura Publisher, I slowly began to reopen the desktop door. Having become, by now, a deeply dependent IBM addict, I ordered a copy of Ventura Publisher version 2. (I had a copy of 1.1 on the shelf; I had tried it but abandoned it for many reasons.) By now I owned a 386-based machine, along with a dozen other IBM compatibles. My company was doing everything on a computer. I decided it was time to reenter, at least tentatively, the DTP arena.

Although I had now accumulated more than 1,000 hours with DTP systems, learning Ventura was no simple, automatic task. Like Pagemaker, it is powerful — but that, by necessity, means it is complicated. And like Pagemaker, it forces the user to play with a mouse and waddle through the user interface (or for DTP addicts, the abuser interface). That meant pulling down a menu which had a menu which had a menu.

Looking back, I'd say I personally became comfortable with Ventura after investing roughly 100 hours into the product. You might do better or worse, depending on how quickly you grasp things — like your mouse.

(With another 100 hours concentrating on customizing the program on a technical level, I also became quite expert at loading "foreign" fonts into the program. That gave me the ability to load widths from any typesetting system, but that is a far more complicated topic than this book could address.)

Picking and choosing

It's no secret that my company specializes in magazine and catalog preparation. So, do we use DTP for all of our tasks?

No. Certain jobs have too many one-shot variables. For example, we might have to set a brochure for a magazine client. Will the design of the brochure match the "tags" or design parameters of the magazine? Not likely. So if it appears that it would take more time to write "custom tags" for every conceivable difference between the brochure and the magazine, we just might put it directly on the typesetting machine, and use conventional typesetting code to set the job.

But if you don't *own* conventional typesetting equipment, how could you do that? What if you owned only a copy of Pagemaker and only a Linotronic L-300? How would you set a one-shot job? It might be far more time-consuming than you dreamed. And while Pagemaker has a reputation for allowing faster one-shot changes, the Ventura user might face investing a large amount of time into a very small, otherwise simple typesetting job.

So in our case, we allow our operators to decide whether to put a job on the system, or directly into the typesetter. Virtually all of our repetitive accounts (magazines and catalogs) benefit from DTP, but many of the little jobs go right into the typesetter with conventional code. The ability to go either way is a luxury we have because we come from the "typesetting side" of the business. If you enter from the DTP side, you will have no other choice but to follow the instructions, tag your text, and sometimes waste a great deal of time doing a very simple task.

DTP as a drug

Looking back, I question my decision to invest those thousand hours into that horrible system, a concept that was full of holes. Each hour I spent in front of that screen, each minute that I tried to work around another bug, I could feel myself sinking. I had a bad feeling that it wasn't working. Why didn't I stop? What the heck, is there nicotine in DTP?

I can now see the problem more clearly. Here's how I got addicted:

- I believed the sales claims. It did not occur to me that I was being lied to.
- I assumed, therefore, that I could implement the software.
- When I began to fail, I blamed myself. After all, I had seen demonstrations, and "this thing worked."
- I chose to address the problem, which now appeared to be some personal weakness or stumbling block. I would stay with it.
- I did not pick a cutoff point.

I'm a fast learner with a very strong background in typesetting equipment and terminology, and I have about 5,000 hours of computer experience of one sort or another. If I had picked a cutoff point of 500 hours, I'd be 500 hours ahead. Likewise, some users out there will simply *never* be able to make a DTP system work, just like some people can never ride a bike or fly a plane.

Without some sort of master plan and check/balance system, you run the risk of doing what I did: Trying to make something work that, for whatever reason, can never work. In my case, it was the software itself. In another case, it might be the hardware — or the operator. Trust me: All three have to work together, or nothing happens. You need an educated operator, good software, and hardware that can deliver what you expect.

It would be wise, then, if whenever one person was expected to learn or install a DTP system, that another person monitor the investment of time, the quality of the output, and the total time frame allotted before the concept is (1) re-evaluated or (2) implemented on a functional scale.

Summary

- Create a master plan before attempting to install a DTP system. Use a ladder approach, and attempt to achieve a single goal at a time. Forget the sales claims.
- Evaluate jobs. Don't assume that all typesetting can be performed on a DTP system. Look for repetition and uniformity. At the early stages, when in doubt, do it the old way.
- Give one person the task of monitoring progress, but not learning the system on a functional level. That might lead to accidental addiction.
- Pick a cutoff date for reevaluation or implementation.
- Be willing to admit a mistake. There are other DTP products which may meet your goals better, regardless of time you have already invested. There is other hardware. There are even experienced DTP operators on the job market.

Chapter 8:

Output, the Great Equalizer

There are strange stories to be told about the speed of DTP output devices. One I heard from a local vendor. We were talking about graphics and photos, and I asked if they had done time-tests on their L-300.

"Well, yes and no. We had one page that had several photos on it, 133-line I believe. So we were going to time the output, and we started about 1:00 p.m., and quit about 5:00 p.m. as usual."

"So," I said, "it took four hours. That's incredible."

"Well, we never finished. We just turned the machine off at 5:00. We never bothered to try it again, because we had no way of knowing whether the machine had hung up, which we suspect, or whether it was really going to take that long. In either case, at the end of four hours, we didn't care."

I thought that was funny until we were doing some simple tests with our own simple little Laserwriter. I asked

Ken and Joanne what they found when trying to output a test halftone.

"Twenty minutes, I think," Ken said.

"Well, that's not usable. But it isn't bad. Let me see the sample."

"No, that was 20 minutes until we turned the Laserwriter off," he said.

"Why'd you do that?" I asked.

"Because you said do a test, but don't let it sit there all day if it hangs up. I thought it might be hung up, but the light was still flashing, so maybe it wasn't. But I figured after 20 minutes you wouldn't want the machine tied up."

Well, I couldn't argue with that. I'm not about to pay Ken or Joanne what I do so they can eat crackers as they stare at the Laserwriter, which seductively blinks its little yellow light when it's busy doing something important.

Finally, I was at a hardware demo at one point, and the salesman gleefully told a woman DTP shopper that she could put all of her photos right on the screen, run proofs, and do her 32-page weekly shopper, all with the equipment sitting on his demo desktop.

"Show me some sample photo output," she said.

Twenty minutes later, she said, "This is ridiculous. I have 64 pages in an issue. Thanks, but I have to go."

I stayed a few more minutes, asking the salesman what he thought the problem might be. He said he thought maybe the Laserwriter got hung up, and offered to reset it and try again . . . and I left.

What is a normal speed?

In the typesetting business, before DTP, we never got too excited about output speeds. If a manufacturer claimed that his device could set 100 lines per minute of 8 point text, 11 picas wide, you figured that he was probably exaggerating by at least one or two hundred precent, and that you could expect maximum speeds of 25 to 50 percent of the claim. But laser machines changed all that.

When you purchase a laser proofer, and it has a rated speed of eight pages per minute, can you expect to get 25 percent of that speed on a regular basis?

Maybe — but only if you limit your use of fonts, and only if you use no graphics, no tints, no complex line art, no photos. Nothing fancy at all.

If you do perform complex output, you will find that rather then set 8 pages a minute, the machine might set a page in 8 minutes. In fact, not long ago that was published (as someone's opinion) as the generally accepted average per-page speed of the typical laser typesetter or proofer. One page in eight minutes.

What if you publish a 96-page weekly "home showcase," one of those newsprint tossaways that you find in the grocery store? Add graphics and a few handfuls of photos per page, and what have you got: possibly 96 machine hours to run your pages. That's more than two weeks of running time for your weekly, and possibly less, and possibly more. Nobody knows.

Sound outrageous? It's not. Nobody would use DTP to produce a 96 page flyer that had photos in it, low quality or not. That can be done far faster by shooting auto-screening

Polaroids, and pasting them into position on the boards. If you want to generate the type and rules on a DTP system, more power to you. And if that's all you do, you'll probably get very effective, practical output speeds.

Output, then, might be considered the Great Equalizer. Sure, you can "Do It All with DTP." Just like, given enough time, that legendary room full of monkeys and typewriters would have written *War and Peace*. But why wait?

So how do you measure output speeds if you can't find a person with the patience to wait until the page comes out of the machine? You don't need to. You don't need, or want, to know that it will take 30 minutes or 4.12 hours to set a certain kind of page. What you need to know is, what was on those pages that made them go so slow?

Quit doing that

So if you want to quit hitting yourself in the head with a DTP hammer, here are the things to avoid:

- **Photos.** Forget them. There are faster, cheaper, better ways to do photos. Ask your printer, or a professional publisher.
- **Complex drawings.** My former employee, Frank, was a map freak. He drew maps of the U.S. (and the world), in amazing detail, with software of his own creation. A typical map, if you let Frank have his way, might be 500K in size, and require 9 minutes just to send to the Laserwriter (at 9600 baud!). And that assumes that the machine has nothing else to do, like rotate text, paint tints, or load fonts.

- **Tints and patterns.** The more you use, and the more varieties you use, the more you slow down the machine. You can start by losing a minute, but could lose as much as — well, whenever someone turns off the machine.

How does the question of output speed get answered by those who sell DTP hardware? Let's ask Smilin' Jack, our used L-100 salesman:

"Yeah, there's a relationship between what you put on the page and the final output speed. No, I don't think we have any samples we could run here right now, but we'll send you some."

Get that demo in person. And block out plenty of time.

Astounding problems

And now, as promised, a review of some of the more astounding problems associated with output.

Did you know that what you draw on your screen, and what you proof on your Laserwriter, and even what you see as a nice, *color* laser proof may be *impossible* to run as film or paper on your final-output device? It has to do with the way your Laserwriter handles memory compared to how the Linotronic does the same.

While that may soon be solved (with a version 49.3 upgrade, they say), how did it affect the heavy-duty DTP artists in the past? They sent their artwork for final output, the Linotronic locked up, and nobody knew why. The solution? More ghastly than you might think. The drawing had to be modified. Simplified. *The DTP artist had pushed the machines too far*, and had to modify his work into something easier to output.

How do you know when that kind of trouble will pop up? You don't. You experiment. And if your "experimenting" is done as you rely on an outside service bureau for final output, it's not too difficult to imagine how that situation quickly becomes a DTP nightmare.

Now, recall the interview with the art director in Chapter 2, when you learned that one poor DTP user gets one kind of color on his screen (mixing color "matches"), and a completely different color when the job is proofed from the Linotronic negatives.

Finally, recall the artist's comments in Chapter 2. Even when his drawing came out of the Linotronic as expected, it was technically impossible to print on a lithographic printing press. It required absolutely perfect registration, and litho presses typically register only to a thousandth or two. Although this DTP designer supplied "final film," the only way to guarantee it would print in registration would have been to generate a new set of film without tints, and use contacting procedures and handwork to fix the problem.

Even "simple" things can get out of hand. Suppose you need to purchase (and learn to use) a special "filter" to get text from your favorite word processor to the DTP program. On the DTP screen, you make changes, mark paragraphs, etc. But then the editor decides he needs to do a final check and a light re-write. Do you then "filter" the program back to the word processor of the editor's choice? In some cases it is merely difficult. In others, it will be impossible, forcing you to either get the editor onto the DTP computer, or start from scratch.

Believe it or not, even spacebands can create problems that seem too stupid to be true. If your DTP program "honors" spacebands at the ends of paragraphs, it may sometimes put a blank line where you didn't expect one: between paragraphs, where the phantom spaceband resides. So you might remove them all on the screen. But if an editor later modifies the text in a word processor, his program might put them all back in again. Impossible to solve? No. Aggravating? Very. And what about double spacebands? "Real" typesetting equipment often removed them automatically. Your DTP system may think it's okay to run two in a row, creating another task for the operator.

The astonishing reality: Your artwork may be impossible to output to film. It may come out in the wrong colors with the wrong fonts. It may not be printable. And you may get stuck with "one way" editorial movement, into the DTP system but not back out to the editing system. No *wonder* some of the early DTP users are now former users!

DTP in real life

How does DTP output stand up to conventional typesetting equipment? In order to make a fair comparison, we have to limit the DTP system to straight text and rules — but then, we have to decide which conventional system we want to compare it to.

In the "real" world of typesetting, there are machines which set type as slowly as 10 lines per minute (about 10 characters per second) and those that set up to 10,000 characters a second (over a page a second). Obviously, DTP cannot be compared fairly to both extremes, which are separated in total cost by roughly the same factor that separates their abilities.

The only way to fairly evaluate and compare speeds is to take dollar figures and apply them to similar situations.

Let's take low resolution and $4,000. How does the DTP laser proofing device stand up? Terrific! There is nothing in the world of conventional typesetting, used or new, which — for $4,000 — could output a page of rules and text.

So let's move up. What does $20,000 in DTP output get you? Possibly, one of the newer, paper-only, 600-DPI laser proofing devices. However, for many applications, the quality of the output on these machines is suitable for final reproduction. Remember, a 300-DPI machine has a resolution of 90,000 dots per square inch. A 600-DPI device has a maximum theoretical limit of 360,000 dots per square inch. So it is not twice as good. It is four times as good. And that's good enough for certain users.

Again, there is nothing in the conventional market (non-DTP hardware) that could even remotely compete with that system. True, the 600-DPI installation could not produce film output at this stage of the game (that may change), but it still wins. There's no competition unless . . .

What about a used typesetting machine, for example a Mergenthaler 202 running film output via a Postscript emulator program? Could it outperform the 600-DPI setup? In many cases, yes it could. In other cases, no. It would depend on several variables, including the expertise of the operators, the cost of the used machine, and whether film was an option or a necessity. But just to keep the picture fair, there are ways to spend less than $20,000, create your pages on a computer screen, proof them on a laser proofer, and run them on a typesetting bargain like the 202. But don't run out and buy your first piece of "old" typesetting hardware based on that possibility. The only firms which are successfully running Ventura and Pagemaker output on 202's and 8600's are typically those firms which had owned the equipment previously, know what they're doing, and have the expertise to maintain, manage, and modify a complex working environment. If you're new to typesetting and page makeup, this isn't the choice for you.

Finally, let's go to the $40,000 to $80,000 level. Would you purchase DTP equipment, or comparable "conventional" typesetting equipment? More than likely, you will end up with both. The typesetting manufacturers have all given up, and all recognize that to sell more hardware, they need DTP compatibility. Once you rise toward the $80,000 level, you are in the "new real world" of typesetting. While you might think that the professionals don't recognize DTP, they almost have no choice. DTP output will run on any of the new typesetting devices. Likewise, the machines will accept other coding formats. But for practical purposes, consider the full-blown typesetting system in the $40,000 through $250,000 range to be DTP capable.

How about the speed of this new equipment? Does it compare to the "old" technology?

In some cases it runs faster, and in some cases slower. Whenever you take a page to the limit (photos, patterns, tints), you will get an immediate and drastic slowdown for your efforts, and few in this business would encourage you to attempt such output. In fact, if you run enough "slow" pages through your service bureau, you'll soon find out what their hourly rate is (forget the $8 to $12 figure they quoted for text). It might be $50 to $100, and a single page just might take that long.

The high end

What about machines that are more costly still? What are the other output options?

At present, the next frontier appears to be marrying small DTP systems to large, multi-million dollar setups, such as the Scitex color system. Here's how that might work.

You set your pages up on your screen, leaving the photos and art and color work to be inserted later. You send this material to your big, we-got-one-of-everything printers. He loads your material into his Scitex. Meanwhile, he scans your B-W and color photos, and makes them available to the Scitex computer, too. Then he puts it all together on the screen: Type, photos, rules, tints, you name it. The next thing you see is a color proof of your publication.

Pretty fancy, huh? You bet. But with a few million dollars in hardware, a staff of 20 researchers and technicians, and a lot of guts, you, too, could go into the High End of DTP. Is anyone doing it?

Sure. There's an aggressive printer right here in my home state of Wisconsin marketing that concept. They have the firepower, the money, and the staff in place. As I write this, the entire setup is in the early stages — but if they succeed with it, rest assured others will follow suit.

Output and color

That brings up a point. Should the average small user or department attempt to get into color output? Should you consider buying one of the new-fangled scanners, and doing your own color corrections right on your Mac?

I would strongly suggest that if you are so dead set on getting your color generated electronically, that you seek the services of someone (like the printer I mentioned) who is not trying to do it with $15,000 of hardware and a staff of one, but who is investing the millions it will take to get that technology to perform in the real world of printing. Like many DTP siren calls, color is out there, but it is Hacker Color as of this writing. It is not practical in the professional world, where real color separations are purchased for little more than the cost of film and equipment depreciation.

Summary

- In some cases, DTP components have been so incompatible that you could proof a job but not run final high-quality output.
- In certain cases which require use of a program to convert a specific word processing format for the DTP system, the result could be single-direction work flow, making further editing on the word processor difficult or impossible.
- Usable output speeds of DTP systems are best measured on the practical level of text and rules only. More complex material is unpredictable, and most professionals don't run such material on their DTP systems, anyhow.
- While DTP is capable of producing photos, no person or firm interviewed for this book, nor any acquaintance of the author, routinely outputs photos or other overly complex material as of this writing.
- The future of professional DTP growth may lie in its integration with the more expensive, faster, more capable systems, such as the Scitex color system.

Chapter 9:

Doc, Will I Be Able to Play the Piano?

You know the old piano joke, don't you? I can't remember if it was given to us by Groucho or Henny, but it goes like this. A man goes to his doctor. He learns he'll need a serious operation. He asks, "Doc, when I come out of surgery, will I be able to play the piano?" The doc says, "Sure." The man says, "That's wonderful. I've always wished I could play the piano."

And so it is in this business of Desktop Publishing, or (as I prefer to call it) Tabletop Typesetting.

Here's a typical formula for generating "off key" typesetting and page makeup.

Our ingredient list starts with a few presumptions: Typesetters are overpaid, artists are creatures of whim who slowly work by the hour at exorbitant rates, and if the average person simply knew how to use the mechanical tools of art and typography, the average person could do it all alone. Faster. And better. Yeah.

To that, we add a computer. Not just your everyday, hit-the-right-button computer, but a computer designed to be operated by a chimpanzee. Instead of assuming the chimp can type, this computer assumes the chimp can only point. At art and stuff. In fact, this computer tells the monkey when it can have its disk back. Not the other way around, like a real computer.

Now we add two typefaces. True, those of us who've lived and died with typesetting for the past 20 years know there are maybe 20,000 typefaces, each with a special twist or quality. But for the chimp, we need only a typeface with feet, and a typeface without feet. Later, when the mini-gorilla learns that two faces do not a publication make, we'll have a market for Gil Sans Outline Extended Backslant, and other things we couldn't get off the shelves until the revolution. But for now, two faces will suffice.

Now we toss in some words. Embolden is a nice word, isn't it? Let's tell the monkey that when text should be "darker," he should point at **Embolden** (honest, I did not make that up). And some commands: Click and Double-click. The little primate should understand those, right? When you want something, you click. When you want it right away, you double click.

Finally, we complete the hardware recipe with a typesetting device which has approximately six percent of the resolution of a typical professional machine. (Surprised? 300 spots or dots or lines per inch gives you a maximum density of 90 thousand pixels or points or whatevers per square inch. On a real typesetting machine, 1200 line resolution offers a maximum of over 1.4 million little dots per square inch. Of course, some typesetting machines can go to 2400 line resolution, which is 5.76 million specks in one square inch. But then, what do monkeys know about math?)

And there you have it. The recipe is complete, and we'll soon start seeing nasty little output. Because our new "artist/writer"is so anxious to "publish," we'll see pages popping out of that laser printer within hours, just like the advertisements said. But our new publisher will be making the same, stupid, silly, fundamental mistakes that you and I made before we went to school. Atrocious as these may seem, the errors will fall into the following general categories:

Lack of typographical sense. While any device can set a bullet, a minus sign, or a degree mark, the novice may not know (1) that there are such things, (2) how to get at them, (3) or when to use them.

- So you see special paragraphs starting out with a hyphen instead of a bullet. You see - - two dashes used instead of an em-dash. You find ellipses...all crunched together, instead of being spaced out according to (1) the fixed space theory or (2) the variable space theory, both of which I defend depending on who says what first. You see 2-line drop cap initials that don't reach the ascender of the first line — sort of like midget drop caps. Unbelievable as it may seem, you see the same quote marks used to open and close a quote. You never see a double prime. And a single prime? The desktop publisher will think you're talking dirty.

In addition, you'll occasionally see two spaces between sentences (a no-no in real type), and underlining when italics were called for.

Lack of editorial ability. What do editors really do, anyhow? Just read stuff? Ah, our desktop monkey has no use for editors. So nobody reads this particular stuff critically. And of coarse (sic), that leads to thinks (sic) that the spelling checker cannot fine (sic, sic, sick!). Worse yet, is that a sentence or paragraph may have no meaning: Example. See?

Lack of fundamental design skills Okay, graphic applicant. Recite the golden rule of visual division. Thank you. We'll call you. Next.

But you serious designers out there either read, or learned, or instinctively knew, that dividing an area with roughly a 1 to 3 ratio provides a pleasant feel. On the other hand, making a square 10 percent wider than it is tall rips at the very heart of even our graphic designer chimp. How come nobody *tells* you this stuff?

Yet when our graphic monkey needs 58 percent of the space for one thing, and 42 percent for another, he divides the space like that, and figures "it just wouldn't fit any other way."

Overindulgence in fonts. When we finally do sell some additional fonts to our desktop person, the natural response is to use them, all the time, on every task. And if possible, to modify them. Put shadows around Avant Garde Extra Light, condense Helvetica Expanded Bold, or backslant Garamond Italic.

Underindulgence in fonts. Oddly enough, the opposite sometimes occurs. Instead of using all available fonts, the novice decides to play it safe. So he or she uses one font in one size. The result is one of those little 2-1/4 by 3-inch ads in the back of your typical computer magazine. It is set in either Times or Times Bold, probably eight point. The headline is capped, and the text is not. That's it.

Low res output. One would not assume that the average, intelligent person would spend three thousand dollars on a page of advertising in a magazine, but then try to save $20 by not having it run on a high-resolution device — would one? Ah, but we're not talking logic here, nohow.

Enter the desktop designer-publisher-writer. Suddenly, the guy who can't figure out that his pixel density is six percent of the norm figures that he or she can save 6.6 percent of this advertising cost by using low-resolution laser output — even though virtually every other advertisement in that magazine will be generated with high-resolution equipment. And because this person's eyes have become detuned to quality, that low-res proof looks "almost" as good as real expensive typesetting, hey? Off it goes to the magazine.

Attempted solutions

Of course, the DTP "industry" has attempted to solve these routine gaffs. When you buy certain programs, they come equipped with "style sheets," electronic clip art, and the promise that if you just use the formula approach to design and art, your work will look professional.

That, of course, is an insulting joke to the real pros. Artists have always been able to purchase clip art from whoever that weirdo is who fills books with the stuff. Designers have always tastefully stolen the work of better designers. Complete magazines have been designed to look like other, good-looking magazines. But somehow, in the professional world, we don't steal so obviously that we get caught. We don't "clip."

Same with writers. There are only so many words in the language, and far fewer that have meaning to the average person. So we all use the same ones. We just use them in a slightly different order, and we get away with it, most every time. By applying DTP theory to writing, we might as well just use "clip articles" (what us pros refer to as filler, fluff, or advertising revenue).

What would it all take?

What kind of skills are actually required to generate professional-looking design and layout? Ah, but we've already made an assumption. Who says it must look professional? Lots of DTP output is far from professional looking, right?

But let's assume that you *do* want your material to look professionally designed. Can you expect one person to perform all of the tasks? How much training would be required to get consistent, professional results?

Unfortunately, that might be asking too much. Let's examine the business in the days before the DTP machine. We had persons who specialized in typesetting, and persons who specialized in design and layout, and persons who were hired for verbal skills, and even persons who did nothing but check things. Each was a professional. But it was very rare to find a single individual who could do several things, like professionally set type, and then professionally design a page. Why? Because one job is far less structured than another. A person with the meticulous nature required for accurate typesetting is often not the person with creative, bright design skills.

In some DTP environments — particularly those which are installed and used by only one person — it is no surprise that a job which reads well and has no spelling errors also looks terrible. Or that a job which looks quite professional has lots of typographical errors. Or that a job is simply mediocre on all counts.

The point to remember is that if you seek professional output, you must start with professional skills. It is rare to find three or four professional skills in a single individual — and rarer still to find meticulous skills, creative skills, and verbal skills all in one individual.

Reality

For good or bad, you can't "can" aesthetics, creativity, or taste. A DTP system can dole out a bit of kerning and a touch of indent, but the program has no brains. You can design a package, but you can't package a design.

Professional designers and writers have always been able to work with or without sophisticated tools. Certain DTP equipment (and software) makes the professional's job easier, but does not make the professional. Design is in the head. Creativity is in the soul. And like an X-acto knife or scissors, desktop publishing is on the desk.

Summary

- DTP equipment and software does not guarantee professionally designed and printed products.
- A thorough understanding of design, typesetting, editorial, and other publishing functions can't be purchased. It comes with experience. Bad design can be created with a pencil or a computer.
- To play the piano, you must practice the piano. The same holds true for writing, artwork, layout, design, and all of the other disciplines associated with professional publishing. Computer experience is an additional skill — not the only skill.

Chapter 10:

The Good News

I'm sending out a press release when I finish this book. I can just see the trade journals print it, word for word. Look for it under the headline, "Desktop Publishing Saved My Baby." And I don't consider that to be any more outrageous than the other things DTP is supposed to be capable of.

You, though, are no fool. If you read what came before this chapter, you're going to look at DTP with both of your skeptical eyes open. And you will be armed with some critical opinions, shared by this author and by many of us who have installed DTP systems. A few notable summaries:

- Desktop Publishing is not publishing. It is hardware and software which allows the operator to use a computer to assist in typesetting, layout, and design tasks.
- DTP does not install itself and train its operators. Someone installs it, manages it, trains people. You might plan on 100 hours of training (or low productivity hours) per operator.

- DPT cannot outperform conventional typesetting on all levels. This is because DTP's strongest features revolve around repetitive formats or parameters.
- Scanned photos and the use of complex graphic elements have potential applications only for low-quality publications, in-house reports, or other non-professional material.
- No professional firm interviewed in the research of this book, and no acquaintance of the author, currently uses scanned photos in conjunction with a DTP system.
- Output speeds (low or high resolution) are directly tied to the complexity of the page. Type, boxes, rules and panels are fast. Tints, photos, and graphics, can cost minutes or even hours.
- To achieve professional results, the DTP operator needs a professional comprehension of typesetting and layout. Generally that means the DTP system must be staffed by at least two persons.
- The "complete" DTP system would cost millions. Rather, you install limited DTP workstations, dedicated to specific tasks. Then, a DTP station can be installed for $3,000 to $8,000.
- The concept of merely sending your output to a service bureau has holes in it. The bureau must have access to the fonts you use, and the font numbers must match or be temporarily mapped.
- Fonts aren't free. Plan on $200 per basic family of Roman, Italic, Bold and Bold Italic. If you don't buy fonts, you're stuck with only those few which come with the system.

The Good News

- Output can be expensive. If you had all your material run as DTP film, you might spend a minimum of $48 per page plus lithographic stripping and proofing for a total of $100 or more (using color). A conventional or mixed approach might be cheaper.
- Corrections and alterations can be as expensive as generating a page from scratch. You may have to completely rerun four pieces of film in order to change a single word.
- Output devices aren't cheap. If you decide to purchase a high-res output device instead of using a service bureau, plan on $40,000 to $85,000. The lower cost machines are virtually unproven.
- DTP is not inherently faster than a pencil and paper. A simple two-page spread can take two minutes or eight hours, depending on which software is used, and how efficient the user is.
- Alcohol, nicotine, and DTP are all addictive, and in the event of abuse, withdrawal is rarely spontaneous. Someone must monitor the DTP environment, measure its efficiency, and set goals.
- DTP has tremendous inertia. Once the decision is made to install it, it tends to snowball on its own. Again, critical management skills must be employed to continually evaluate it.
- Changes are routine. Plan on some retraining and upgrading every year; sometimes every six months. While "old" typesetting companies tended to see major developments every few years, DTP users see monthly changes.
- Editorial is not addressed in most DTP circles. The skills of the editor, copywriter, proofreader, and others in-

volved in "meaning" (rather than typesetting or design) are as necessary for DTP environments as they are for conventional environments.

In other words, kids, DTP is no panacea. It doesn't "do it all," it isn't always faster, it is not easy to learn, it doesn't make pictures, and it can't produce publications. Or to put it in as few words as I can, Desktop Publishing isn't. (I wish I new where I read that!) So what good is it?

The complete DTP approach

There are certain environments which might benefit from a "complete" DTP system. Suppose, for example, that I work in a large office building, and I deliver a daily news report to all of the office tenants.

If my little report requires me to print photos of the tenants, and quality is not the issue, and I must include news right up until 5:00 a.m. yet deliver office-machine copies to the tenants by 6:00 a.m., and — for some reason — I must have better than typewriter quality, then a compete desktop system might be in order.

The fact is, it is very difficult for me to come up with a very sensible example. Why? Because the "complete" DTP system handles photos, graphics, and anything else which might appear on the page. It handles those elements with slow speed, low quality, and great cost in computer hardware.

But somewhere, somehow, there are little niches in this world which require every bell and whistle that DTP can jangle or blow.

Limited DTP installations

But when you take away the things it does poorly, DTP can leave you with a mighty impressive typesetting, layout, and even design engine.

Consider that today's DTP system can automatically kern and track, can hyphenate and justify text faster than virtually any dedicated typesetting front end, and gives the operator stunning, automated control over tasks that once (1) either took hours, or (2) were impossible.

Consider that today's DTP system allows the publisher to view material on screen, hyphenated, even in the true font, even including kerning and tracking.

Look at proofs. Only a few years ago, the publisher would send a disk to the typesetting firm, the firm would run line-printer copy, the editors would read it, the typesetter would make corrections, the galleys would be run, copies would be made on an office copier, someone would tape and cut and move things around. Then, typesetting technology evolved to the point that the full page could be generated on the screen and set in one pass. And finally DTP came along with its cheap and instant laser proofs.

When you couple an instant proof with a cheap computer, you have, for $8,000 or so, what type professionals spent $250,000 on — just a few years ago. And the reason they spent that money was to be able to build pages on the screen — the same reasons a publisher might want to install DTP.

With a simple DTP system, you can draw perfect boxes and rules. Those who have cleaned a mechanical pen more than a few times know the benefit of that!

And all of these typographic and layout benefits don't even begin to address DTP's strong suit: What the DTP people call "tagging." For example, throughout this book, while writing it, I made my word processor put the tag "@SUBHEAD = " before every subhead. When the DTP system got hold of it, it treated all of those subhead "paragraphs" with the same custom typesetting attributes. Dozens of factors could be programmed into the subhead "tag," such as whether I want them kerned, what kind of tracking I want, the space above them, the space below them, the font, the size, the space between multiple subhead lines, whether they will be indented, centered, or flush right, whether a subhead will be hyphenated if necessary, how many minimum lines must appear below it at the bottom of a column, whether there will be space above it if it appears at the top of a column . . . are you getting the drift?

All of those parameters were addressed for my particular subheads in this particular book. I can have an unlimited number of "styles" available to the DTP system at any time, and subheads are only one "paragraph style." I can have a virtually unlimited number of paragraph styles in any given working environment.

The reality is, if you understand how complicated all of this stuff was before DTP, you begin to appreciate the typesetting power in DTP. True, we achieved the same output before DTP arrived. But not at the same low cost, and not with the same power, and not even with the same speed. Not for less than a half million dollars, anyhow.

This same incredible versatility of DTP is what can make it so hard to comprehend and professionally execute. Sure, the old time typesetters know when and where to use kerning and tracking, and that there are specific ways to handle each customer's subheads. But the newcomer to DTP must eventually comprehend a virtual avalanche of sophisticated ability — a bigger mess of automatic ability than we typesetting pros ever dealt with in the past.

Don't get me wrong. I've spent thousands of hours looking forward to this environment. I've spent years waiting in the wings, hoping someday to say, "This stuff works." But without the preceding nine "Warning Chapters," I didn't feel it appropriate.

Reverse technology

As I said in the introduction, I use DTP tools. I used them to paginate this book. I just don't use them all.

As a final thought, I might mention that some of us in the typesetting business have done a bit of reverse engineering. While DTP systems routinely speak "foreign" languages, such as Interleaf, PostScript, or Hewlett Packard, many of us in the business have hundreds of thousands of dollars invested in "old technology" and conventional fonts.

While we could chuck it all and buy fancy-dan PostScript imagesetters, in many cases it isn't required. Some of our customers need only type and rules. In fact, as I've pointed out, that is what DTP generates best, anyhow. So, we've seen the emergence of software which takes a language, like PostScript, and converts it to another language, like Cora (a typesetting language).

I have personally written such a piece of software, and while it was no easy task, it wasn't insurmountable. When

PostScript is doing the easy, fast stuff—no photos, no tints — it merely says, in its own bizarre fashion, to put this word or this letter this far up the page, this far over, in this typeface. For a computer programmer, it's a relatively straightforwared task to convert PostScript units (or any other units) to picas and points, and to translate the other appropriate commands into their typesetting language counterparts.

The result? We haven't all tossed out the old technology just yet. If the promise of photos and art comes a bit closer, and if more customers find it practical to build the entire page on the screen, the old 202s and 8600s will have to go. But for now, in many cases, these old dogs are spitting out pages of text, complete with boxes, rules, panels, tracking, kerning, and whatever, just like the imagesetters. These machines were fast not only in their own day, but today, too.

Which software?

The strong contenders in DTP software are, in my opinion, and as of this writing, Ventura Publisher for the IBM PC, and Aldus Pagemaker for the Macintosh. I do not mean to say that I would recommend Pagemaker for the IBM PC, either. I specifically mean exactly and only what I said. If you have an IBM, buy Ventura, and if you have a Mac, buy Pagemaker. If you have neither, my personal preference is Ventura on the IBM, but that is based largely on inertia. I currently use it, and the more I use it, the more I like it. I suspect the same things happens to those who started with Pagemaker on the Mac.

There are other programs, by the way. QuarkXPress for the Mac is certainly popular, and its many users are happy. But to be honest and lazy at the same time, I can't review every DTP system in detail, and the best ones will rise to the top in terms of popularity and sales. That they have, and these three lead the pack.

Word processor connections

You may have read about DTP word processors. Basically, these are word processors which can make pretty fancy pages and output to a laser printer. Some of them, for example, can include charts, graphics, and even photos.

The potential for being mislead here is that some persons think they can have their editors generate galleys right on the screen with, for example, Word Perfect, and then import those galleys into Ventura or Pagemaker. That would take some considerable trickery, and would not necessarily be a smart choice. Remember, DTP software sort of "assumes" it will be allowed to rehyphenate, to kern or track (depending on the way it's set up), and that if changes are made on the page, text will be rejustified and reflowed. By attempting to "freeze" the galley before feeding it into the system, you defeat that purpose.

My recommendation is to avoid word processing software that tries to get too fancy, or hints at being a DTP word processor. Rather, use any word processor that your editors are comfortable with. I'm familiar with PC-Write, Wordstar, Q&A Write, and several others. They're all fine, but my favorite is PC-Write. It's a fast workhorse, and it (like Xywrite) is one of the few truly "open architecture" word processors, allowing for massive modification, control, and customization of the entire word processing environment, including how it finally outputs material to (in this case) the DTP system.

While it would be nice to think that the editor would have the same kind of line endings on his or her screen as you'd later get with the DTP screen, it just isn't practical right now. (At least, it's something most of us have given up on.) It would make more sense to give the editor Ventura or Pagemaker than to teach the word processing program how to *pretend* to be Ventura or Pagemaker.

Training

It's no surprise that DTP training centers sprang up as soon as DTP arrived. Consider the poor secretary: Her boss buys her a Mac and a Laserwriter and Pagemaker. He says, "I saw on TV that we can do our own publishing, so here. Publish me this report."

Now all she needs is (1) basic typesetting skills, (2) basic editing skills, (3) basic design skills, (4) basic art skills, and (5) nine lives during which she can learn each of these professions. For goodness sake, people get college degrees in each of those areas!

On the other hand, the documentation that comes with these programs might be sufficient for the person who already has extensive knowledge in one or more of those areas.

Suffice it to say, though, that some animals learn faster than others. Some persons will invest 100 hours on their own time, and become virtual experts on their systems.

Others will, sad to say, spend 100 hours trying to get a headline tag to work properly. It's that second animal that needs all the training there is (or better yet, training with a mop or broom, and a new career). So don't hesitate to send your crew off the Ventura or Pagemaker school. Xerox runs their own schools all over the country.

As an alternative, consider either a temporary or full-time employee with prior DTP experience.

What about DTP consultants? I'm one. And I do not recommend you hire one. Sure, I'd recommend myself, but I choose to believe I'm one of those rare consultants who won't sell you a bill of goods. For example, I lost one DTP consulting job because, during the interview I said, "You know, it sounds to me like you don't want to know IF you should get a DTP system. Sounds to me like you just want someone to tell you which one. What if I recommend you don't buy a system at all?"

And with that, they picked a different consultant. Within weeks, they ordered a truckload of Macs. And if the whole mess doesn't work the way they hoped? They'll blame the consultant, of course. (And guess who's money it was! It was a government installation.)

So if you really want a consultant, keep in mind that you're paying $2,000 or so per day so that if the whole mess falls apart, your scapegoat is at a distance, and nobody gets the axe for making a stupid decision. That's the way the consultant game works.

Off to the store

So there you have it. Nine chapters of warning labels, and one lousy chapter of praise. It was an ugly job, but somebody had to do it.

When you do understand it, and are disciplined enough to use only those functions that are practical, and are willing invest a few hundred hours in making it work, DTP is a typesetting marvel, a fantastic proofing system, a terrific design device, and a whole lot more. It offers more power, and is probably more complicated, than professional typesetting systems of the past, but that's a benefit to the professional — not a detraction.

"So, Mrs. Lupton. Just how DID Desktop Publishing save your baby?"

"Well, I have this Macintosh, and I'd just recently published a list of our local emergency phone numbers, and I'd put that publication on the wall near my phone. That very next day, my baby somehow got at the medicine cabinet. Well, if I hadn't used that 18 point Swiss Bold for the Poison Center, I just don't know WHAT would have happened...."

Summary

- Desktop publishing cannot save your baby.
- You do not "publish" something by setting it in type.
- You have been successfully de-programmed. You can now function in the world of DTP hype without fear of being brainwashed. Congratulations.

About the Book

The publishing industry has never seen the likes of DTP hype. As mentioned in the book's final chapter, it is impossible to make up claims that are any more outrageous than those we have already seen in print. Yes, DTP can even save your baby.

Mixing humor, wit, sarcasim, and his 25 years of typesetting and print production experience, the author examines the claims one at a time, sorts the reality from the promise, and gives the reader an honest taste of DTP as it is working in the field, today.

DTP isn't all bad. It is merely one more production tool in a long evolution of printing hardware and software. It has its place. This book puts it there.

Editing & Production

The text for this book was written on an IBM-compatible AT computer and a portable Zenith XT-compatible computer (used while the author was on the road). The word processor and spell-checker was PC-Write version 3. Pagination was performed with Ventura Publisher version 2 on an IBM AT-compatible computer and a 386-clone. Proofs were run three separate times on a vintage Apple Laserwriter. Each set of proofs took approximately 30 minutes.

All computers used in producing the text had at least 20 megabytes of hard disk storage. The type widths for the fonts (Times family) were loaded from Mergenthaler tables into Ventura ".WID" tables. Widths were from the CRTronic series.

Final output was generated on typesetting film, on CRTronic digital typesetters using VP40, a conversion program written by the author and distributed from Parnau Graphics, Inc. Stripping was conventional.

About the Author

Jeffery Parnau has lectured and written extensively on the subject of print production, from typesetting through bindery. In 1985 his first book, *The Handbook of Magazine Production*, was published by Folio Publishing Corporation, Stamford, CT. His views on the industry have appeared in many trade journals over the past decade. He has also served as a consultant to major print purchasers in the U.S. and abroad.

Parnau also founded Parnau Graphics, Inc., in 1978 in the Milwaukee area. That firm specializes in magazine and catalog typesetting and film preparation, using both conventional and contemporary technology.